RAILS TO BANFF, MACDUFF AND OLDMELDRUM

THREE GREAT NORTH OF SCOTLAND RAILWAY BRANCH LINES

DUNCAN MCLEISH

Published by the

Great North of Scotland Railway Association

2014

This typical branch line scene shows an up train arriving at Rothie Norman in the 1920s. The signalman is about to exchange tablets with the fireman, milk churns wait to be loaded and a few passengers are ready to board the train. Local trains such as this would soon loose out to road transport.   (GNSRA)

A mixed train leaving Banff in Great North days. The line approached the town close to the shore and ran behind the fishermen's cottages. The station site itself was cramped; there was not even enough room for a run-round loop so the locomotive would back out of the station, uncouple from the coaches and then draw forward into the other platform. The coaches would then run under gravity into the station. A short extension ran to the harbour but was little used.   (Gordon Series postcard)

Contents

Acknowledgements

The author would like to thank GNSRA members Mike Cooper, Ross Kerby and Graham Maxtone for contributing illustrations and is especially grateful to Keith Fenwick for the massive effort that he put into editing the book. Thanks too to others who contributed illustrations.

© Duncan McLeish 2014
ISBN: 978-0902343-26-9

Published by the Great North of Scotland Railway Association, www.gnsra.org.uk
Printed by **Berforts Information Press, Eynsham, Oxfordshire, OX29 4JB**

Front cover : The branch train for Banff waits at Tillynaught in July 1964. The man platforms were at the other side of the building, which by then had lost much of its roof. Although this was just before closure, the service on the branch was as good as it had ever been as it provided connections with all the trains along the Coast line. The branch was also the last outpost of steam in the north east, all the other services had been dieselised by 1961. Locomotive haulage on the branch ensured that freight traffic could also be handled but the low level of traffic did not justify a diesel loco with steam heating boiler.

(Mike Stephen)

A postcard sent in May 1914 of Turriff shows part of the station in the foreground with the road to Oldmeldrum and Aberdeen in the background. This was a time when the railway was still the main means of transport but road use was starting to build up, a process which would accelerate after the Great War and lead to the eventual closure of all the branch lines described in this book.

The Oldmeldrum branch train waits at Inverurie in the bay platform on the left as passengers from the down service transfer. The branch train is headed by a class B 2-4-0 and consists of a 6-wheeled full brake, a 4-wheeled composite dating from the 1870s and a 4 or 6-wheeled third built in the 1880s. The train on the right is headed by a class C 4-4-0 and again consists of non-bogie stock so would have been a stopping train. The photograph was taken between 1902, when the new station at Inverurie was opened, and 1909, when the last of the Class B locos were withdrawn. The loco heading the branch train was always referred to as 'Meldrum Meg'.   *(George Washington Wilson 144,467)*

Chapter 1

Introduction

At first sight Banff, Macduff and Oldmeldrum may seem to have little in common with each other. But all three were served by branch lines that were ultimately owned and operated by the Great North of Scotland Railway. All three towns are in what is now Aberdeenshire Council's area, though Banff and Macduff were, until 1975, in Banffshire, whose county town was of course Banff. They all tended, and still tend, to look to Aberdeen as their business and service centre, to which transport links have always been of great importance.

The rail links to Aberdeen were not particularly direct, especially so in the case of Banff, 64 miles by rail from Aberdeen, while Macduff was 50 and Oldmeldrum 22. As railway passenger and freight rates were normally charged per mile, distance could later become a factor when competition from road transport materialised. However, the real transport artery between the three towns and Aberdeen is the A947 road, by which the distances between Aberdeen and Oldmeldrum, Macduff and Banff are about 18, 46 and 48 miles respectively.

One might ask why a railway was not built between these three places directly towards Aberdeen roughly along the line of the present A947 then along the coast from Banff to Elgin; a route currently served by regular and busy bus services from Aberdeen. The physical difficulties would have presented problems but these would not have been insuperable. There was certainly rail traffic to be had, for inland Aberdeenshire is rich agricultural country. Turriff, on the Macduff branch, and Oldmeldrum were once important market centres. Moreover Banff, Macduff and other towns along the Moray Firth coast were, and in some cases still are, important fishing centres which were to provide much trade for the railway. The answer to the above question lies at the very dawn of railways to the north west of Aberdeen.

Even before the main line from the south, the Aberdeen Railway, had been opened in 1850, thought had been given to the lines which would continue communication north from Aberdeen. The ultimate target was Inverness. At that point a direct link between there and Perth seemed a distant prospect, so the primary aim was to establish the rail link to the Highland capital via Aberdeen.

In 1845 the main contenders to build such a link were the Great North of Scotland Railway competing with the Aberdeen, Banff & Elgin and the Inverness & Elgin Junction Railways. The former, projected more or less over the present line between Aberdeen and Inverness, was to have a branch from Grange, near Keith, to Banff and Portsoy. The latter inovlved one company from Aberdeen to Elgin via Turriff and Banff and a separate one thence to Inverness. In the parliamentary contest that followed the Great North of Scotland was victorious, its act gaining the Royal Assent on 26th June 1846; at the time it was the longest railway thus far authorised in Scotland.

Also at that time there was talk of promoting a Great North of Scotland (Western Extension) Railway linking Inverurie to Elgin and Banff via Oldmeldrum and Turriff, close to the turnpike road, later the A947. This desirable link seems to have been promoted mainly by local interests.

The Great North would have been involved no doubt, but any interest quickly evaporated during the financial problems which beset that company almost as soon as it had obtained its act. It was in no position to support such a lengthy branch, far less a secondary main line. One must realise then that the branch lines were promoted in piecemeal fashion and according to the cheapest option currently available, without any regard for an overall strategy for building railways in the area.

It is not within the scope of this volume to discuss the problems, financial and otherwise, which beset the Great North in its early years. These are admirably dealt with by Peter Fletcher in his book *Directors, Dilemmas and Debt*. It is sufficient to say here that the company had great difficulty in building its main line even as far west as Keith; from there rail traffic was to be taken onwards by a generally hostile company, the Inverness & Aberdeen Junction Railway, later part of the Great North's rival, the Highland Railway. It took until June 1854 for the line to be opened over the 40 miles from Kittybrewster in Aberdeen to Huntly, and October 1856 to reach Keith.

By that time the Great North was unwilling, and indeed unable, to devote any of its scarce resources to the building of branch lines, however desirable. According to its chairman, Sir James Elphinstone, the Great North was emphatically against promoting branch lines, but would provide limited financial support to the local promoters; those lines, when opened, would in turn channel traffic to the main line of the Great North, which would thus recoup its original small investment. Unfortunately all this did not turn out quite as Sir James had planned, as we shall see. The first branch line to be promoted and opened was that to Oldmeldrum, which we shall now look at.

The epitome of the rural branch line. An ex-North Eastern G5 0-4-4T No.67287 ambles along the Oldmeldrum branch near Lethenty in July 1952 hauling a modest goods train. The brake van is an ex-GNS vehicle. A few of these ex North Eastern locomotives worked in the north east in the 1940s and 1950s, after the native 0-4-4Ts were withdrawn.   *(J L Stevenson)*

Chapter 2

Oldmeldrum Branch until 1922

The Inverury and Old Meldrum Junction Railway

In November 1840 the appropriately named Rev George Garioch wrote about contemporary Oldmeldrum for the *New Statistical Account of Scotland*. At that time the town was known as Old Meldrum, and the parish as Meldrum. The name is probably derived from the Celtic Mealldruim, which means the shoulder or ridge of a hill; this seems to be borne out by the local topography. 'Old' may have been a corruption of allt, a stream. Mr Garioch was writing only a few years before railways were projected in the area.

The picture he draws is of a busy little market town in an agricultural area. Oldmeldrum had been created a burgh of barony in 1672, and its population in the 1831 census was 1,790. Its inhabitants enjoyed a 'good weekly market for provisions', and hiring fairs in May and November. About one third of the parish was uncultivated, but much of the rest was used to rear the Aberdeenshire breed of cattle, 'much approved of in the southern markets'; Southdown, Leicester and also Scottish hill sheep were raised. Produce was mainly oats, bringing in £9,268 per annum, and turnips £2,964. In addition there was the knitting of worsted stockings, two weaving shops and a brewery; and later a distillery.

Such commodities of course required transport when not sold locally. Since 1804 Oldmeldrum had been situated on the Banff to Aberdeen turnpike road. There were stagecoaches and twice daily mail coaches on that route, and two carriers provided cartage to Aberdeen. For fuel the peat moss had almost been exhausted and coals had to be carted from the harbours at Aberdeen and Newburgh. The turnpike 'which offers both an economical and expeditious mode of travelling' had stimulated industry and the building of houses in the town; 'the general aspect of the country is much improved'. However, the arrival of the Aberdeenshire Canal at Inverurie, while certainly benefitting the Garioch area as a whole, probably drew some trade from Oldmeldrum market to that of its rival a few miles away.

Altogether then it was a reasonably prosperous picture and one which presented a promising prospect for a railway. Let us look now at the *Third Statistical Account of Scotland* with its record of Oldmeldrum, written in February 1955, again by the parish minister, Rev Kenneth Macmillan. The preamble to the Aberdeenshire volume had noted the part played by laird and farmer in promoting the 'new' farming, 'which was the county's part in the industrial revolution'. However, the Aberdeenshire farmer also 'remains faithful to the turnip'. Stock rearing was still important, but with less emphasis on the Aberdeen–Angus breed of cattle. There was some dairying, and the rearing of pigs, sheep and poultry. Mr Macmillan notes that in Meldrum parish half the available ground was under crops, while the rest was grass and grazing. He also notes that the Oldmeldrum population had been at its highest in 1861, namely 2,343, while in 1951 it was 1,670; about the same as in 1831. The local market had been transferred to Inverurie in 1921, which probably did not do the branch line any good, though the GNSR locomotive works at Inverurie employed about twenty people from Oldmeldrum.

On the face of it then Oldmeldrum seems to have been much the same in 1955 as it had been in 1840, though with small but significant changes. In 1955 the branch railway from Inverurie to Oldmeldrum had been closed to passengers for more than twenty years, though freight services still had another ten years to run. In the 115 years since 1840 the Oldmeldrum line had come and almost gone; Mr Macmillan dismisses it in barely a line of his account. However, 'an excellent bus service now serves those living on or near the main Banff–Oldmeldrum– Aberdeen road'; the A947 again. The nearness of Aberdeen 'with frequent and cheap travel facilities' had changed the way of life in Oldmeldrum. So did the railway to that place have any effect? Let us now turn to its history to find out.

While a branch railway to Oldmeldrum had not been envisaged in 1846 when the Great North was considering its strategy in the area, it was the first branch from that company's main line to be promoted and completed. It seems to have been regarded by Oldmeldrum's inhabitants as a means of restoring the town's trade, which had been affected by the opening of the Aberdeenshire Canal to Inverurie in 1796. A committee was eventually formed under the chairmanship of the magnificently named Beauchamp Urquhart of Meldrum; its vice-chairman was John Manson, a local banker, secretary James Chalmers and engineer John Willet. Seven of the nine directors were locally based, while two represented the legal profession, whose members often appeared on railway company boards. Its secretary was James Chalmers, whose minutes of the company's proceedings have, unfortunately, not survived.

These local worthies then had to raise the £22,000 required to build the Inverury & Old Meldrum Railway; this was to be offered in £10 shares. Though the Great North participated by subscribing £2,000 to the construction of the line, it did not appoint any directors to the company's board. The bill for the line was of course presented to Parliament under the

A postcard issued in GNS days showing the branch train ready to depart for Inverurie. The train consists of a couple of 4 or 6-wheeled passenger carriages, a passenger brake, about 4 wagons and a goods brake and is hauled by 'Meldrum Meg', in this case a Cowan 4-4-0.   *(Lens of Sutton)*

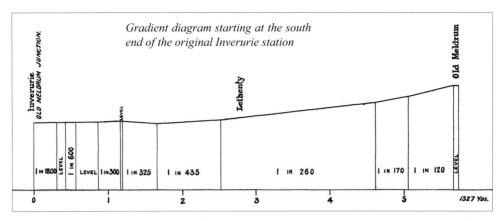

Gradient diagram starting at the south end of the original Inverurie station

contemporary spellings of the two towns, and it became an act when it received the Royal Assent on 15th June 1855 (18&19 Victoria, c65). Among other provisions, it allowed the company to borrow £7,000, one third of the capital stipulated, as was standard in railway acts. Also, while the line was to be locally owned and managed, it was to be worked at cost by the Great North whose normal passenger and goods rates would apply.

At that time Inverurie station was about one half mile south of the present one, the site now being marked by 'Old Station Road'. Though the track diverged from the main line north of the present station, the actual junction was sited just to the north of the original station with the first mile of the branch being alongside but independent of the main line. Thus the branch as a whole was just under 5¼ miles long, but about one mile less from the point of divergence to Oldmeldrum.

The money for construction seems to have been raised mainly locally and, with few civil engineering works of any significance, it was completed relatively quickly and cheaply. While Vallance names the contractors for the line as the reputable firm of Locke & Errington, they were more the engineers whose local representative, John Willet, later became the I&AJ company's engineer. However, much of the work on the ground seems to have been contracted out to the local firm of Milne & Leslie. Construction of the line was completed between September 1855 and the following June, and cost about £5,000 per mile, quite low for the time. Its mandatory inspection was carried out for the Board of Trade by Colonel Yolland, who found all satisfactory and sanctioned the opening to passengers, which took place ceremonially on Thursday 26th June, 1856.

Such an event was early enough in railway history, and important enough in the area, to be the cause of much celebration. The *Aberdeen Journal* gave a lengthy account of proceedings. A special train left Aberdeen with guests from that city. At Oldmeldrum it was met by a cheering crowd, many of whom had been granted a holiday. The station was bedecked with evergreens and placards displaying patriotic and other mottoes. On leaving the train the guests were given wine and cake before proceeding to the Meldrum Arms Hotel. The exuberant locals were meantime given a free return trip on the line to Inverurie.

At the Meldrum Arms three hundred guests dined at four o'clock. The event was presided over by the Company's vice-chairman, John Manson of Fingask, who apologised for the absence of the chairman, Urquhart of Meldrum, who was indisposed. The toasts usual for such an occasion were proposed and drunk. Mr C. Dalrymple, in toasting the prosperity of the little company, expressed optimism as to its future, but pointed out that some facilities, such as those for freight, were not yet ready. He also hinted that the site of Oldmeldrum station

Lethenty looking towards Oldmeldrum. The platform was rebuilt and this building constructed in the early 20th century. The goods siding was on the other side of the level crossing which can be seen beyond the platform.   *(Norris Forrest)*

was less than convenient; it was about half a mile from the town centre. This was to haunt the railway later.

The toasting went on into the evening with just about every concern, person or group connected with the railway being honoured. The Aberdeen guests departed by rail at eight o'clock, while the locals enjoyed a bonfire and fireworks display. The line could now settle down to ordinary business. Passenger trains commenced on 1st July and goods traffic on 6th July. The only intermediate station, Lethenty was opened on 1st October, 1856.

Freight outwards was to be mainly agricultural such as oats, potatoes, milk, livestock and milled grain. Also served was the Glengarioch distillery, which required delivery of malt, barley, coal and wood for barrels, and also transport of the finished product. Coal was brought in for domestic users and for users such as the gasworks, along with seeds, fertilisers and cattle feed for the farmers.

The initial passenger service was four down trains to Oldmeldrum and three up to Inverurie. From the former the line struck out west for about one mile through agricultural land, then turned south and eventually south east to Inverurie. The main intermediate station was Lethenty 2¼ miles from Inverurie. Though open to general passenger traffic, its main, if not sole, freight traffic was from a meal mill, which had its own siding accessed via a wagon turntable.

In the early days, trains also called at Muirtown half way between the farms of Muirtown and Fingask and almost 3 miles from Inverurie, where Mr Manson, the vice-chairman of the erstwhile Oldmeldrum company lived. By 1867, trains called instead at Fingask, a simple platform half a mile further on. The present Inverurie station is about 178 feet above sea level; Lethenty was about 195 feet, Fingask 244 and Oldmeldrum 264: a continuous but not severe climb for down trains.

Traffic seems to have been slow to develop and James Stewart, the Great North's vice-chairman, stated that they had not expected any dividend from the new line; nor did they get any. However, in its first year it had brought £2,500 worth of traffic on to the Great North, which was satisfactory. Even so the local company was unable to pay off its accumulated debts; it had raised only £14,700 of its authorised capital of £22,000. Therefore, by its Act of 1858 (21&22 Victoria c45), it leased the line to the Great North for £650 per annum and was also allowed to issue £10,500 worth of preference shares to clear the debt.

By 1866 the Great North itself was entangled in a web of working and financing several unprofitable branches for independent companies, and its Act of that year (29&30 Victoria c288) consolidated them, including the Oldmeldrum company, into its own concern. Holders of Oldmeldreum preference shares received an equivalent amount of Great North preference shares, but the ordinary shareholders only got £3 of GNSR stock for their £10 shares. Thus the little Inverury & Old Meldrum Railway Company passed unprofitably into history on 1st August, 1866.

The only known photograph of Fingask is one which appeared in the Glasgow Bulletin *on 26th May 1926 under the heading 'A Station without a Staff'. The site of the station is just beyond the crossing on the left in the photograph below. The platform is just visible in the 1900 OS map to the left of the MP.*

Site of Findgask, looking towards Oldmeldrum in October 1954   *(J L Stevenson)*

D2420, a 204HP Barclay diesel mechanical shunter, at Lethenty collecting a number of containers on flat wagons on its return from Oldmeldrum in 1960. The wagon turntable in the foreground connected to the Mill. The level crossing is behind the photographer.   *(Norris Forrest)*

A GNSR Branch

What did the Great North get for its money in 1866? It got a single track branch line with a terminal station at Oldmeldrum. Inverurie had two through platforms, and a bay for the Oldmeldrum branch trains. Locomotives could also be turned at Inverurie on a turntable moved there from Inveramsay. At the terminus there was a single platform to the north of the terminal line, with a turntable at the town end; that had gone by 1887 as there was not room to enlarge it. There was a two engine locomotive shed with carriage accommodation, reached by a siding trailing from the down side, and a small goods yard trailing from the up side. Until the installation of the telegraph in 1885, trains were just worked according to the timetable. In between the two main stations Lethenty could handle passengers, parcels etc, and had some accommodation for freight, livestock and horseboxes, as well as the mill siding. Fingask was an unstaffed halt. Passengers had originally to pay the fare to Oldmeldrum if travelling from Inverurie or Lethenty if going in the other direction, but in latter days tickets were issued to the halt. Passengers joining there were issued with their tickets at Lethenty or Oldmeldrum.

As to train services, these had become four each way by 1860, the service being based at Oldmeldrum. These departed from Oldmeldrum at 8.40 (mixed), 11.30am (passengers and parliamentary), 12.40 and 7.18pm (both mixed). Inverurie departures were at 9.05am (mixed), 12 noon (passengers and parliamentary), 5.28 (goods and passenger) and 7.48pm (mixed). The train descriptions are confusing to say the least, but in practice it probably meant that most trains conveyed both goods and passenger vehicles. 'Parliamentary' meant that these particular trains conveyed passengers at the basic one (old) penny per mile rate. Journey times over the branch varied from fourteen to twenty minutes, the differences being accounted for by any freight business dealt with at Lethenty. The service was a self-contained one, and there were

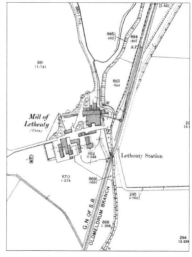

Lethenty from the 1900 OS map. By comparison the first edition map, published in 1870, showed a shorter siding without the wagon turntable and connection to the Mill.

no through trains to and from Aberdeen for instance, though normally there were reasonable connections with main line trains. Nor were there ever any Sunday services on the branch.

We learn from a report to the Directors that in 1870 the affairs of the Oldmeldrum branch appear to have been in a relatively prosperous state. Running expenses, such as fuel, drivers' wages etc, amounted to £350 per annum, while station expenses came to about £250. There were doubtless other expenses, but those should be set against a total income at Oldmeldrum and Lethenty stations of £4,935. Although that figure would have included traffic going off the branch, it would seem that the Great North was at last getting some return from its investment.

By 1880 Lord Aberdeen was complaining about the delays to trains at Lethenty, apparently caused by shunting the wagons on mixed trains. A proper goods shed was proposed to alleviate the problem, but that seems never to have been provided. Lord Aberdeen also proposed a line to Methlick and Auchnagatt on the Buchan section. His supporters included J. Manson and J. Bruce, bankers at Oldmeldrum, who had been concerned in the original company. However, despite a meeting of the GNSR board with the Oldmeldrum interests, the scheme came to nothing.

Even so, the 1880s seem to have brought some changes for the Oldmeldrum branch. The carriage and engines sheds were rebuilt in 1880 following storm damage. Telegraphic control of trains, normal on the Great North, arrived in 1885 at Oldmeldrum. There were now six trains in each direction, departing from Oldmeldrum at 7.25, 8.45, 10.25am, 1.40, 3.30 and

Oldmeldrum between the Wars, possibly before passenger services ceased. When the building was adapted for office use, the central doors were removed and the front section rebuilt. *(Lens of Sutton)*

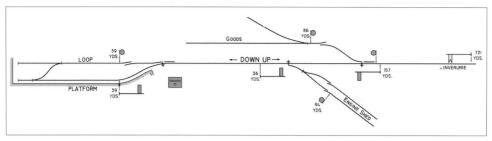

Oldmeldrum signalling diagram 1896. The lever frame had 14 working levers, 3 spares and 2 spaces. A very short run-round loop was provided but that is not shown on the 1900 OS map nor on a pre-1914 postcard. Tow-ropes were used to enable wagons to be shunted to the appropriate siding. (Robert Dey)

5.25pm; and from Inverurie at 7.55, 9.15, 11.52am, 12.30, 4 and 6pm. *Bradshaw* for August, 1887, shows trains at roughly the same times, plus a return trip on Saturday evenings, though an 8.15 return from Inverurie hardly gave much opportunity for an evening's pleasure in that metropolis. All trains called at Lethenty, but confusion must have reigned for passengers at Fingask; one train each way did not stop, some had a mandatory stop and others were stopped to pick up by hand signal from the platform or by informing the guard at the previous station to set down. Timings over the branch were little different from twenty years previously, and show that most trains were still mixed. Even so, it was the best service ever on the line.

Some of the developments of the 1890s were positive ones. In 1895 interlocked signalling came in to use to meet the requirements of the 1889 Railways Act, which promulgated that method along with other railway safety measures in the wake of the Armagh disaster of that year. A new signal box was opened on 3rd June at the Inverurie end of the platform on the down side. Signals were as in the diagram reproduced from the Board of Trade inspector's (presumably retrospective) report of July, 1896. The Old Meldrum box, which was classified in the sixth level of the Great North hierarchy of signal boxes, had fourteen working levers, with

Oldmeldrum station, in later days. The signal cabin still has its nameboard. There were further sidings to the right.   *(GNSRA Collection)*

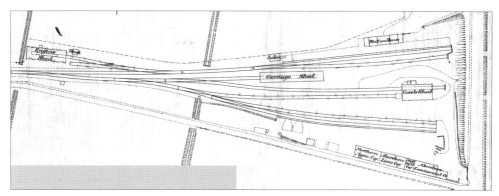

LNER plan of Oldmeldrum dating from after the passenger closure; it has been annotated in light pencil to show tracks to be removed. The layout is that same as that shown on the 1900 OS map. The Carriage Shed opposite the signal box had been added since the 1870 map together with the siding just south of it.

two spares and two spaces. As services declined in the 1920s, the box was reduced to a ground frame in 1927, but survived until the total closure of the branch in 1966. From the 1890s too the wooden station building, which replaced the original one, has also survived, but is now at Milton of Crathes on the Royal Deeside preserved line.

Bradshaw of December 1895 shows a small decline in the number of services provided over the branch, with five each way from the first departure from Oldmeldrum at 7.25am until the last arrival there at 6.36pm. Two trains had a mandatory stop at Fingask, the rest were stopped by 'sig'. The Saturday evening services had disappeared. Timings were 15-17 minutes for the journey, which suggests that trains were no longer mixed. That is confirmed by the 1901 timetable, which shows five passenger and two goods train trips each way daily. The goods departed Oldmeldrum at 11.15am and 3pm, and returned from Inverurie at 12.25 and 3.30pm. The time taken was twenty minutes in each case, so little work was allowed for at Lethenty. The two goods trains were fitted in between passenger services, and were presumably worked by the Oldmeldrum based engine and crew. The Saturday evening passenger return trip had been restored, however. On 8th February 1902 the new Inverurie station, nearer the town centre, was opened. This effectively made the branch about half a mile shorter, and a minute or two here and there was cut from schedules.

An enquiry in 1903 into the financial situation of each of the company's lines gives statistics for the twelve months to 31st July 1903. From these we learn that the Oldmeldrum branch produced 54,012 passenger journeys, which brought in £912. Freight traffic produced 589 trucks of livestock and goods and minerals accounted for 65,962 tons, which netted £1,415. Thus the branch brought in a total of £2,366 in that year; rather less than the 1870 figures quoted above,

	INVERURIE TO OLDMELDRUM—DOWN TRAINS.								OLDMELDRUM TO INVERURIE—UP TRAINS.						
		1	2	3	4	5	6	7			1	2	3	4	5	6	7
Miles.	STATIONS.	Mixed 1 & 3.		Mixed 1 & 3.	Mixed 1 & 3.	Mixed 1 & 3.	Mixed 1 & 8.	Sats only Pa.1,3.	Miles.	STATIONS.	Mixed 1 & 3.		Mixed 1 & 3.	Mixed 1 & 3.	Mixed 1 & 3.	Mixed 1 & 3.	Sats only Pa.1,3.
		a.m.		a.m	p.m.	p.m.	p.m.	p.m.			a.m.		a.m.	p.m.	p.m.	p.m.	p.m.
	Aberdeen—*de.*	7 0	.....	10 20	1 15	3 10	4 55	7 10	..	Oldmeldrum *de.*	7 25	.....	10 10	1 35	3 30	5 25	7 25
	Keith—— ,,	6 10	.....	9 10	12 55	.....	5 0	.....	3	Lethenty——	7 33	.....	10 20	1 45	3 40	5 35	7 35
..	Inverurie —— ,,	7 55	.....	11 10	2 30	4 0	6 20	8 15	5¾	Inverurie —*ar.*	7 42	.....	10 30	1 55	3 50	5 45	7 45
2¾	Lethenty ——	8 5	.....	11 20	2 40	4 10	6 30	8 25		Aberdeen— ,,	8 35	.....	11 55	3 15	4 20	6 40	9 0
5¾	Oldmeldrum *ar.*	8 15	.....	11 30	2 50	4 20	6 40	8 35		Keith——— ,,	9 33	.....	11 46	3 30	.....	7 25	9 15

FINGASK PLATFORM.—Nos. 1 and 6 Down and Nos. 1, 3, and 6 Up Trains will stop at this Platform. Other Trains will stop only when a request by Passengers is made to the Guard at the Lethenty or Oldmeldrum Stations, or when Passengers are upon the Platform to be taken up.

Passengers alighting from Down Trains must hold Tickets to Oldmeldrum, and from Up Trains must hold Tickets to Lethenty, which the Guard will check and collect, delivering the collected Tickets at Oldmeldrum and Lethenty respectively.

Passengers joining the Down Trains pay fares from Lethenty at Oldmeldrum, and those joining the Up Trains will be supplied with Tickets at Lethenty, and at same time pay fares from Oldmeldrum. Guard must point out such Passengers at the respective Stations. (W.O. 78/686.)

Timetable for September, 1886

Two of the buildings of the group on the south side of Oldmeldrum station site shown on the plan opposite survived in 2004. The Aberdeen Commercial Company's warehouse is on the left while the short extension to the right was used by the North of Scotland Milling Company. Since then, the section on the left has been converted for commercial use with an L-shaped extension on the right.   (Keith Fenwick)

though other unknown factors may have been involved. Certainly the bulk of its revenue was attributable to freight traffic. From the same set of statistics we learn that the Oldmeldrum branch traffic staff consisted of two station masters, one clerk, three porters, one signalman and one guard, indicating that the Oldmeldrum complement was stationmaster, clerk, signalman, guard and two porters; with a stationmaster and porter at Lethenty. Locomotive staff on the branch was two drivers and one fireman. The latter shovelled 410 tons of coal into his firebox, at the rate of 38 lbs per mile, in a total mileage of 24,414. That accounted for 19.87d (old pence) per mile. Oldmeldrum's earnings were barely £2,000 per annum, which left a surplus of about £500, about 4d per train mile. That represented an operating ratio of expenditure to income of 81%, or 2.18% on the initial investment. The Alford, Macduff and St Combs branches did better, while the Banff, Speyside and Boddam ones fared worse.

At about the same time we get another picture of the branch from the Railway Clearing House *Handbook of Stations* for 1904. From it we learn that Oldmeldrum could handle traffic in passengers, parcels, goods, furniture vans, livestock, horse boxes and private carriages by passenger train; one suspects that some of these traffics were a rarity at Oldmeldrum. Its crane could handle 1 ton 5cwts. Fingask (Platform) handled passengers only, while Lethenty did not handle furniture vans or private carriages; nor did it have a crane.

The GNSR Working Timetable for 1911 shows that the goods trains had disappeared, and that three mixed and two passenger trains each way were again the order of the day. Arrival and departure times were much the same as a decade earlier; in general the timings were still fifteen minutes for the passenger trains and twenty for the mixed. The Saturday evening return trip had survived, however. The timetable also gives arrangements for those wishing to use Fingask Platform; and informs us that 'A through van with Milk Traffic is to be forwarded daily from Oldmeldrum by the 5.55pm Up [passenger] train'. Van and empty churns were to be returned next day on the 1.20pm mixed train from Inverurie.

Another snapshot in words of the Oldmeldrum branch at that time appeared in the Great North *Review* (Nos 5 p52 and 6 p64). A.M. Hardy, who was first acquainted with the line in 1915, describes the journey from Inverurie to the terminus. The train crossed the River Urie on a cast iron bridge of fifty feet span, then climbed through the Cuts of Balhoggardy to Lethenty. At that station were usually some parcels and freight, and milk cans; and a little shunting might be done. Mr Hardy could not remember a stop ever being called at Fingask, with its 'little wooden platform on the port side, and its sentry box at the Meldrum end'. At Oldmeldrum the path up to the town was just that, not the later paved road. His tales of the branch's locomotives and the accidents they had will be detailed later.

That account was of course of a time just at the start of World War 1. The Oldmeldrum branch seems to have been relatively unaffected by the conflict; its problems were perhaps to begin after the war ceased. For on the cessation of hostilities the armed forces released, at low prices, a large number of motor vehicle chassis, which could readily be turned into buses and lorries, and the men able to drive them. Though the Great North itself had pioneered railway operated bus services in extension to its rail system, none of these featured at Oldmeldrum. Its main traffic was to Aberdeen rather than Inverurie. Rail traffic to Aberdeen involved an indirect run to Inverurie and a change of train; always inconvenient, however good the connecting services might be. On the other hand, the bus services that were established by local entrepreneurs could take passengers direct from the centre of Oldmeldrum to the centre of Aberdeen via what became the A947; there was no need to negotiate the steep hill to Oldmeldrum station nor to change carriages. Though buses were generally slower than trains, the latters' speed was negated by the inconveniences mentioned above; bus fares were also generally lower.

The Great North's last working timetable, from 2nd October 1922, showed that there were still five return trips daily: three mixed and two passenger only. The arrangement for milk traffic still applied. Timings over the branch were still twenty and fifteen minutes respectively, and at arrival and departure times which had hardly changed over the decades. Rail timings between Oldmeldrum and Aberdeen were in the seventy to ninety minutes range; this could normally also be achieved by bus. Not that this was to be a concern of the Great North for much longer, for by the Act of 1921 the GNSR was amalgamated with various other companies in Scotland and England to form the London and North Eastern Railway (LNER), becoming its North Scottish Area. The branch's fate under the new and subsequent regimes will be discussed in chapter five.

Oldmeldrum loco shed in September 1935, by when it was out of use. A sleeper across the track prevents access to the shed and the water tower. The shed was still in use in 1932, when the engine stabled there ran through the wall at the opposite end. A photograph of the mishap appeared in the Aberdeen Weekly Journal *on 24th December under the title 'Wayward Meldrum Meg'.*

(W A Camwell)

Inveramsay was the junction for the line to Macduff. It was opened for the branch and closed to passengers when the branch service was withdrawn. The main line platforms are on the left. Macduff trains used the far side of the up platform. Beyond it are the exchange sidings which in later years, as most likely in this photo, were useful for storing wagons waiting to go to Inverurie Works. A light engine is about to set off towards Macduff in this view from the 1930s. (LGRP, GNSRA collection)

Wartle, the first station on the branch, looking north with the Station Master and his family posed on the platform. The style of dress suggests the 1920s, although the Station Master has a winged collar to his shirt. The level crossing at the north end was protected by home signals; the GNSR lower-quadrant up home remained until the line closed. (D McRae/GNSRA Collection)

Chapter 3

Macduff Line until 1922

Although the branch line from Inveramsay to Macduff was built in three stages, and reached the Banff and Macduff area after the Banffshire Railway opened to Banff itself, it will be treated here effectively as one line, as indeed was originally intended by its promoters. Its initial promotion preceded that of the Banffshire Railway, its first section being authorised on the same day as the Oldmeldrum branch. The considerations which have already been described constrained the Great North from promoting the Macduff branch.

The Macduff branch left the GNSR main line at Inveramsay, nearly four miles north west of Inverurie. Apparently a line from Inveramsay would give better gradients than one starting at or near Inverurie. Even today there is no real settlement at the former place, and since Inveramsay station opened and closed on the same dates as the branch line, it can be inferred that the station produced little local traffic; its main purpose was as an 'exchange' station between the main line and the branch, though unlike Cairnie Junction it was never referred to as such.

The first station on the branch was Wartle, which served a scattered farming community, and passenger figures at any rate must have been low. Less so at the next station, Rothienorman, which served what is now a sizeable village. In earlier days the village name was often rendered as Rothie Norman and the station spelling varied over the years. Whatever the case, Rothie was part of Fyvie parish; and indeed the Fyvie ministers' accounts in the *New* and *Third*

Wartle featured on this postcard taken pre-1914. The station staff and possibly a few other people stand to be photographed. Churns of milk wait on the platform to be collected. There are barrows on the platform and a set of ladders to enable the lamps to be lit and trimmed.   *(GNSRA collection)*

An up train approaches Rothienorman in the early years of the 20th century watched by a large group of passengers and staff. The village is to the left and the main station building just visible on the down platform. Trains shunting the sidings here blocked the level crossing but that was only over a minor road. A later view from the same position is reproduced on page 2.　　　(Postcard, J L Stevenson collection)

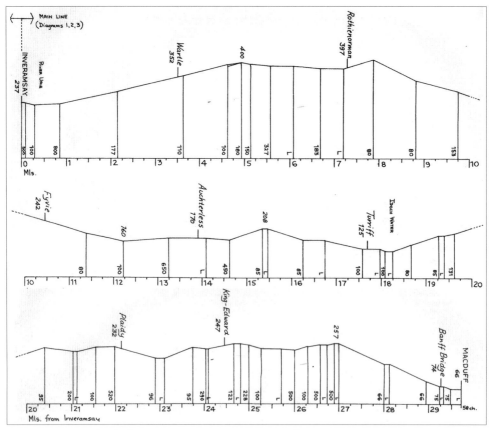

Gradient diagram for the line to the 1872 terminus at Macduff.

Statistical Accounts make little mention of it. Rothienorman station also served rich agricultural country, which would have boosted the freight traffic on the line.

Fyvie itself is now also quite a considerable village. Indeed it was at the centre of one of the biggest parishes in Aberdeenshire. In the *New Statistical Account*, of February 1840, the Rev John Manson informs us that Fyvie had once been a burgh of barony, from before 1400 till sometime around 1700. The town thereafter seems to have gone into decline, though the parish as a whole had 3,252 inhabitants in the 1831 census. The name Fyvie was derived from the Gaelic Fia chein – deer hill; and there is a hill of that name nearby. In 1840 agriculture was its main industry, with oats bringing in £22,785 per annum, and turnips £8,125; cattle and sheep were also reared. Provisions had to be carted from Macduff, Newburgh or Aberdeen. The roads were maintained by the landowners, but were in good order, and the arrival of the Aberdeenshire Canal at Inverurie had helped to stimulate trade in the area.

In the *Third Statistical Account* the Rev Ninian Wright noted that arable farming, and stock raising, along with dairying, were still important in the area. In 1951 the population of the parish was 3,006. Unusually a fair account of the railway is given. The GNSR branch had 'greatly increased amenities of country life, bringing coal to rural communities for the first time, and artificial fertilisers ... to agriculture. Passenger traffic became a profitable source of revenue.' However, after World War 1 bus services were started by Bert and William Giles of Fyvie and carriers turned to motor lorries. Now Alexander's buses were operating sixteen return trips per day to Aberdeen. It can hardly have helped the railway that Fyvie Station was about one mile from the centre of the village. Indeed 'Fyvie Station' was recognised by the Post Office as a separate settlement. It was however, closer to one of the driveways to Fyvie Castle.

The next station on the line was at Auchterless, which means the cultivated field on the side of a hill; that is borne out by the topography of the parish, which in 1831 contained 1,706

This view from the rear of a Macduff-bound train in 1960 shows the layout on the south side of the level crossing at Rothienorman   *(Keith Fenwick collection)*

Fyvie looking south. The station was close to the A947 but some distance from the village. The crossing loop was an early casualty and was taken out of use in 1936.   *(GNSRA collection)*

people. Cattle were raised, along with sheep. Oats and milling were important in 1840, and peat and turf were dug; coal had to be carted from Banff and Macduff. The parish population in 1951 was 1,208. Aberdeen-Angus and shorthorn cattle were still reared. The railway had closed to passengers and 'goods trains are few and far between', but there was an hourly bus service to Banff and Aberdeen. The site was over three miles from the Kirktown of Auchterless.

Turiff was the first terminus on the line. 'Turiff' is apparently derived from the Gaelic for mount or height, which is appropriate to the area; however, some had suggested that it

The main building at Fyvie in April 1952, by which time there was little trace of the loop and down platform. The goods yard is to the right of the platform. The siding is the distance is to catch runaway wagons.   *(CJB Sanderson/GNSRA collection)*

Fyvie building from the approach road. Although taken in August 1988, this view is one of the few showing the 'other' side of the buildings between Inveramsay and Turriff. By this time the building had been adapted for storage. It was demolished a few years later. *(Keith Fenwick)*

meant towers or turrets. Certainly the town is still known locally as 'Turra'. The Rev James Cruickshank in the *New Statistical Account* of 1842 gave the population of the town in the previous year's census as 1,309, with 1,837 living in the landward part of the parish. Turriff had been the scene of the 'Trot of Turriff' in 1639, a skirmish which marked the start of the Civil War in Scotland. About two thirds of the parish was under cultivation, the main produce again being oats, turnips and potatoes. Aberdeenshire cattle predominated and there were some pigs, but few sheep. There were eight fairs annually in Turriff, but no weekly market, and there was a daily stage coach to Aberdeen over the turnpike road.

In the 1951 census in Turriff burgh there were 2,994 inhabitants. It had become a burgh as a result of the Police Act of 1850. The Rev P. Craik McQuoid suggested that the town's name came from Turbruach, the tower on the bank. He also noted that Messrs Hutcheson's Limited were famed for various processed food products, with one hundred lorries on the road. However, he made no mention of the railway, though the hourly Banff – Aberdeen bus services were again pointed out. Also mentioned was the famous 'Turra Coo', which featured when Robert Paterson refused to stamp his new-fangled national insurance card and had his cow impounded and sold by Sheriff Officers, amid demonstrations and protests.

The first station on the second section of the branch was at Plaidy, barely a hamlet, in the parish of King Edward, whose ministers make no mention of it in their accounts. The next station was King Edward itself, whose name had nothing to do with a monarch or a potato! It seems to have been derived from Gaelic words meaning the head of the valley; and there was a ruined castle at the end of the valley. The station was in a hamlet, now called Balchers; the small settlement now called King Edward is about half a mile away. Another form of King Edward was Kinnerward, and locals usually pronounced the name as 'Kinedart'. The *New Statistical Account* gives the population of the parish in 1831 as 1,906. They reared cattle and sheep and produced oats and turnips. Salmon fishing on the River Doveran, ie Deveron, was also important. The only settlement of any size in the parish was at New Byth, on its eastern edge several miles away. The daily Banff – Aberdeen mail coach also passed through

King Edward parish. By 1951 its population had fallen to 1,675. Cattle and potatoes were still important on the farms, which had been much mechanised. The hourly bus service between Banff and Aberdeen had 'spelt doom' to the railway.

The initial terminus was close to the bridge over the Deveron to Banff and so was called Banff and Macduff until 1st August 1866, when it became plain Macduff. It was also referred to in some documents by its location at Gellymill. The line was later extended to Macduff itself when the original terminus was replaced by Banff Bridge. Macduff, with Gardenstown and some other small fishing ports, formed part of the parish of Gamrie, whose population in 1841 was 4,742. Again about two thirds of the parish was under cultivation. Recent agricultural improvements had increased yields, with the cattle and grain going to London by sea. Fish caught by Macduff's fleet included cod, ling, whiting, haddock and herring. Macduff, which had originally been called Down and had become a royal burgh in 1783, had a provision market on Tuesdays. The '-duff' in the modern name comes from the family name of the Earls of Fife, who owned land in the area. Macduff had a daily stage running between Banff and Peterhead.

By 1951 Macduff, as well as still being a fishing port, had also become a holiday resort; the *Third Statistical Account* enumerates its leisure facilities. The population of the parish of Gamrie had now risen to 5,408, with 3,322 in the burgh of Macduff itself. Cattle, sheep and pigs were again raised, along with poultry. The railway is noted as having been closed to passengers in

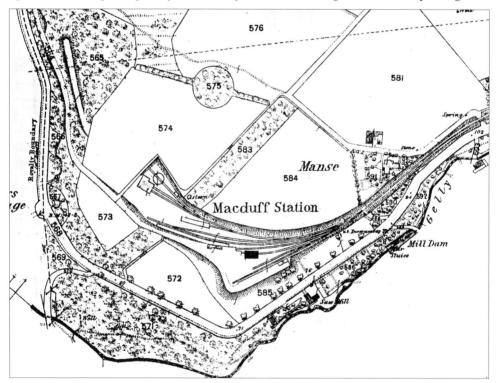

The First Edition OS map, surveyed in 1869 and published in 1871, showed the original terminus at Macduff. Maps of that era did not cross county boundaries, so the bridge itself is omitted. The terminus includes a single platform with a small goods shed to its right. At the other end, the loco shed and turntable can be seen. The narrow building just below the 'M' of Macduff was the carriage shed. Part of the trackbed of the extension to the later station has already been built and can be seen cutting through the wood (565) near the top left.   *(Reproduced with permission of Ordnance Survey)*

1951, due to facing fierce competition from the Banff – Aberdeen bus service; though goods trains still ran.

Such then were the conditions in the area in about 1840, when people were considering the projection of a railway into it; and in about 1951, when the line's passenger services were just being withdrawn. As at Oldmeldrum, agriculture flourished in both periods, with carriage of livestock and produce likely to go by rail; and, although places like Turriff and Macduff were not huge, there was passenger traffic to be had. Macduff's fishing traffic and the Deveron's salmon would also have brought traffic to any railway in that area, though of course sea traffic through Macduff would still be a competitor to the branch. Let us now examine its promotion and operation until 1922.

The Banff, Macduff & Turriff Junction Railway

As noted in chapter 1 there had been early plans to promote a long branch from the main line of the Great North through Oldmeldrum and Turriff to the Moray Firth coast at Macduff and Banff. These had proved to be too ambitious in the contemporary financial climate. Even so, the potential rewards from carrying fish from the Banff and Macduff area, and agricultural produce from its farming hinterland, were interesting possible promoters. So, even before the Great North's main line was opened, consideration was being given locally to promoting a line to the coast. Elsewhere plans were being put forward for lines from the Keith area to Banff and Portsoy.

In October, 1853, the GNSR board heard that a proposal for the line through Turriff towards the coast had been notified by other parties and decided to promote a line of its own. It was a year later before the local group produced a prospectus for their line. However, presumably for financial reasons, it was only to reach as far as Turriff, over a distance of about eighteen miles. The route was planned with a view to lessening gradients and construction costs, and was to be worked by the Great North for 50% of receipts, but with a rebate on any traffic that passed from the branch on to the main line. As we know, the Great North was by that time unwilling to promote its own branches, but it agreed in April 1855 to contribute £40,000 to the local company, despite some mutterings from its shareholders. As a result of these various arrangements, the line received Royal Assent on 15th June 1855 (18&19 Victoria c57) as the Banff, Macduff & Turriff Junction Railway, with a capital of £120,000, with the usual one third borrowing powers in addition.

Its initial board was chaired by Sir James Elphinstone of the GNSR, with five of his fellow directors and two locals; Robert Milne was initially the secretary. The engineer was Alexander Gibb and the contractor John Brebner of Aberdeen, who agreed to do the work for £109,550. Elphinstone, Milne and Gibb occupied similar positions with the Great North. Once construction was begun, and despite the usual squabbles over finances and the contractor's progress, it seems to have proceeded reasonably smoothly, though the navvies' wages had to be increased to attract workers. This may have contributed to the cost of the line rising to £138,000 by 1856. However, by March 1857 the company was able to contract the building of the stations to Robert Watson of Aberdeen. Four months later the passenger service was set at three return trips daily between Turriff and Inveramsay, with connection to three of the four daily trains on the GNSR at the latter place, and one return goods trip. An agreement was made with the Electric Telegraph Company for installation of the telegraph along this line; this was used for regulation of the traffic, in accordance with GNSR contemporary practice. The line was now ready for traffic.

Colonel Yolland inspected the line for the Board of Trade on 6th September and reported that the permanent way consisted of 65lb malleable iron rails laid in lengths of 15ft. They were fixed in cast iron chairs by oak keys. Sleepers were of Scotch fir, 3ft apart and 9ft long by 9in or 10in wide. The ballast was mostly gravel 'but not of a superior quality'. The line was in fair order, so permission to open was given.

On 4th September a special train ran from Aberdeen to arrive in Turriff in time for the customary dinner and other celebrations. Public service began the next day. There were stations at Wartle, Rothienorman, Fyvie and Auchterless. While earthworks had been kept to a minimum, there was a rising gradient from the junction at Inveramsay (228 feet above sea level) through Wartle (at 350 feet) to a summit at Rothienorman (392 feet), before a long descent at 1 in 80 to beyond Fyvie, beside the River Ythan at about 200 feet. Thereafter the line continued on down gradients to Turriff station at 128 feet. Some GNSR stations had their height above sea level added to their name boards.

Unfortunately, as at Oldmeldrum, the traffic did not develop as the promoters had hoped, particularly as far as freight receipts were concerned. In the first year's accounts revenue from the line, along with the GNSR rebate, brought in £7,589, while expenses and interest on loans amounted to only about £200 less. There was still a deficit on the capital account, only £14,000 of which had been raised locally, and it was proposed to issue £20,000 in preference shares to liquidate the debt. An extra passenger train had been introduced in the summer of 1858, but this had now ceased and the service was now three mixed trains each way on weekdays only. It was based at Turriff where there was a locomotive shed and turntable; similar facilities were also provided at Inveramsay which meant that tender locomotives could be used on the branch for the Board of Trade then disapproved of reverse running by tender locomotives.

In 1859 the Company's Act empowered the issue of preference shares and also a change of name to the more logical Aberdeen & Turriff Railway. However, in the current state of

Auchterless from a postcard issued in GNSR days. The box in the distance controlled the level crossing to the north of the station as well as the points at that end. Another box was provided at the south end but that closed when the loop was taken out of use in 1933.   (Graham Maxtone collection)

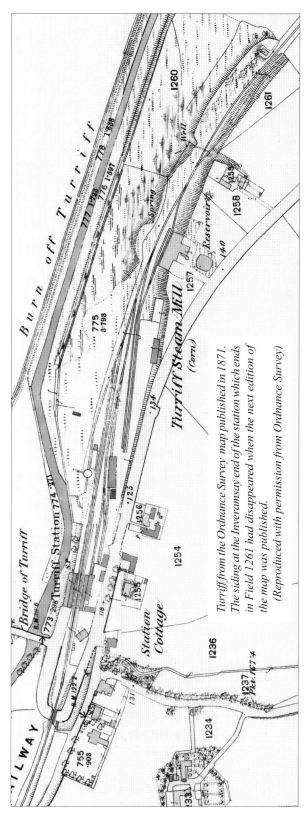

Turriff from the Ordnance Survey map published in 1871. The siding at the Inveramsay end of the station which ends in Field 1261 had disappeared when the next edition of the map was published.
(Reproduced with permission from Ordnance Survey)

the money market, no preference shares could be issued. In the end the Great North did lend some money to the Aberdeen & Turriff, until 1865 when the debt of £32,995 was converted into 3,290 preference shares, taken up by the Great North. After the initial profit, the company lost over £1,000 in both 1859 and 1860, though it made a small surplus in 1861. The same was true of the two following years, but the profits were ploughed into repairing the line. Losses resulted in 1864 and 1865, when the GNSR decided that it would be better for all concerned if it absorbed the Aberdeen & Turriff company, and various other local companies, into itself. The Aberdeen & Turriff agreed to this on 23rd June, 1866.

Banff, Macduff & Turriff Extension Railway

While the original Banff, Macduff & Turriff Railway had fully intended to reach the coast, the money to proceed beyond Turriff could not be raised. However, the idea did not die, and as early as December 1855 a meeting was called at Macduff, where it was felt that a railway was essential to boost the trade of its harbour. It was also felt, possibly correctly, that any line from the west to Banff would do little for Macduff. So it was decided to raise £10,000 to set the scheme in motion for a line towards Turriff, with the hope that the local landowners would be cooperative in supplying land and/or finance for the line.

The line's prospectus of November, 1856, proposed an 11¼ mile extension from Turriff to Macduff, which would be worked

STATION & BRIDGEND, TURRIFF.   GAMMIE PHOTO.

Turriff was the first terminus of the branch from Inveramsay. The station was established on the west side of the town, a short distance away from it. The road to the town crossed the river and went off to the right in this photograph. The line from the south can be seen on the left, running past the signal box and then to the main building which is right of centre. Several cattle wagons are visible in the siding at the end of the goods yard which was to the left of this view.   *(Gammie Postcard)*

by the Great North. The terminus was to be at the east end of the great bridge between Banff and Macduff, and would it was hoped be of service to both towns. Even so, it was one mile or more to the centre of either place. The Banff, Macduff & Turriff Extension Railway bill became an Act on 27th July 1857 (18&19 Victoria c57). The company's offices were to be in Banff. Capital was to be £80,000, with borrowing powers of £27,000. The GNSR was to contribute £5,000 and appoint three directors; there were to be three local directors. Edward Mortimer, a Banff solicitor who had been involved with the first Turriff company, was appointed secretary.

Mortimer, under the chairmanship of W.J. Tayler of Glenbarry, set the project in motion even before the three Great North directors took their seats on the Extension Company board. It then promptly got itself into trouble over finance and dealings with the contractor, George Milne of Kinaldie. Eventually, and after much argument, the Great North directors took their seats and Sir James Elphinstone took over as chairman, though he gave way to William Tayler in 1859. Robert Milne (from 1858) and Alexander Gibb of the GNSR then took over as secretary and engineer respectively.

During all this construction of the line had stopped, with capital slow to come in. Lord Fife pledged £15,000 if other locals promised £5,000, though even that was barely enough to secure progress. In April 1858 the GNSR got the local company to put its house in order and confirmed that it would work the line. So construction restarted, proceeding by spring 1859 as far as Keilhill, that is King Edward. Money trickled in and by April, 1860, enough had been raised to construct the line to a terminus in the vicinity of Macduff; this was in fact to be at Myrehouse, some two miles from the town! By then Robert Watson had successfully tendered for building the stations at Plaidy, Keilhill and 'Macduff Road'. In fact enough money eventually came in to allow the terminus to be placed at Gellymill, some four hundred yards short of the east end of Banff Bridge.

This view of Turriff looking north in 1936 shows how the station building was constructed to enable the line to be extended northwards. There was limited clearance between the buildings and trains, hence the long platforms at the south end which were newer and therefore higher. The footbridge was an LNER replacement for the original wooden GNSR structure in the same location. *(LGRP)*

The intrepid photographer had climbed the up home signal to take this aerial view of Turriff, looking south in August 1956. The road ran under the railway on a tight bend below the photographer, coming from the town on the left and then going past the station towards Fyvie and Aberdeen. The goods yard was on the right beyond the platforms and was accessed from the road on the right. The Steam Mill is near the trees in the far distance. *(John Grant)*

The south end of Turriff in April 1952, with the signal box on the right and the goods yard on the left. The goods shed was behind the photographer. Further back, the Turriff Steam Mill (corn) was served by a siding.   *(CJB Sanderson/GNSRA)*

Opening of the line was delayed by the desire to let the earthworks in the cuttings and embankments settle; there had also been some flooding. In fact the earthworks had not been particularly heavy, but that had only been achieved by having a ruling gradient of 1 in 66, mainly on the descent towards Banff Bridge. Plaidy was about 245 feet above sea level, while Banff Bridge was barely 100. Expenditure on the line had been £72,000, which had been more or less covered by shares and loans. The contractors had complained about late payment, while the company complained about the inadequacy of the earthworks and of the track and sleepers, a not uncommon scenario in railway construction. The line was inspected on 1st June. In this case, the rails were 18ft long and as was previous practice, rails were not joined by fishplates; instead larger chairs holding both rails together were used. The Inspector regretted that the rails were not 'fished.'

Opening came on 4th June 1860 apparently with comparatively little ceremony. While Plaidy and King Edward opened to passengers then, they did not open to goods until March of the following year. A station was proposed at Mountbletton between King Edward and Macduff, but was not proceeded with. The terminus was referred to as Banff & Macduff in timetables until 1st August 1866, when it became plain Macduff.

There were immediate complaints about the rates charged and a demand for a tramway to Macduff, to which the GNSR made some small concessions. While income had been initially successful, there had been a falling off in 1861. Services were four return trips on weekdays only, in continuation of the Aberdeen and Turriff services, and a summer extra was proposed with cheap fares; these were particularly aimed at fishwives from Banff and Macduff who went inland to sell their wares. Journey times over the whole line from Inveramsay to the coast

The station name was displayed on the glass panel above the doors from the platform to the booking office at most Great North stations.

varied between 95 and 120 minutes; however, the service soon reverted to four trains per day. In addition staff reductions were proposed, but not implemented. 1862 brought a proposal for the extension to Macduff proper, with a tramway to the harbour. Though timber traffic did temporarily bring in some extra revenue, the extension proposal was dropped in 1865. Again the Great North was becoming impatient about yet another branch line it was operating simply muddling along under a local board and proposed absorption of the little company. That was approved in June 1866 and the final meeting of the company took place in November of that year.

To go forward a little into the GNSR period: the amalgamation act of 30th July 1866 had also provided for the extension to Macduff being promoted within five years, though it abandoned the tramway. The Great North was in no hurry, but eventually opened the extension to Macduff on 1st July, 1872. The Board of Trade inspection was carried out by Colonel Rich on 28th June. He reported that the line was 62 chains long on a ruling gradient of 1 in 75, with a succession of ten chain curves. Double headed rail weighing 72 lbs per yard was laid on chairs weighing 28 lbs each. These were spiked to sleepers placed about three feet apart; the sleepers were half round and measured nine feet by ten inches by five inches. The curves were laid on single headed rails of 65 lbs on chairs of 56 lbs; these rails were closely paralleled by 'guard' rails of similar dimensions. There was a turntable at the terminus at Macduff, while the station at Gilliemill (sic) along with its turntable would be abandoned. The one small bridge on the extension was of sound construction, but the Colonel wanted some minor improvements at the stations at Macduff and Banff Bridge. There had been landslips on the side of the hill between the two stations and these would require watching. Satisfied that these matters would be seen to, the Colonel sanctioned the opening of the line.

The new station opposite the end of Banff Bridge was appropriately so called, and the original terminus was abandoned on the opening of the extension. Various considerations had led to the line being built around the west side of the Hill of Doune to the new terminus which was on the high ground at the south west edge of Macduff, nearly 150 feet above sea level. Proposals for an extension to the harbour still emerged from time to time, but it would have

The site of Plaidy looking north in October 1954. This was one of the least photographed stations on the line; nothing has come to light which illustrates the station when open. *(J L Stevenson)*

King Edward also featured on a Gammie postcard which showed the rear of a Macduff-bound train. The small goods yard was on the left behind the signal box. (GNSRA collection)

been very steep, and nothing was ever done about it. Perhaps the lack of use on the steeply graded Portsoy harbour branch at this time – it was abandoned in the 1870s – may have turned the Great North against the idea.

Under GNSR Control

By 1872 the Great North had of course been in charge of the Macduff branch as a whole for some six years and had operated it from the beginning. For its money it got a branch line 29 miles long at the takeover, with three quarters of a mile to be added in 1872. The mileage of the branch was reckoned from zero at the junction at Inveramsay and the mileposts were on the down, ie northbound, side of the line. There were stations at Wartle 3¾ miles, Rothienorman 7½ , Fyvie 10¾ , Auchterless 14, Turriff 18, Plaidy 22½ , King Edward 24¾ , 'Banff and Macduff' (closed in 1872) 29, Banff Bridge 29½ and Macduff 29¾ (both opened in 1872). The line was wholly single tracked apart from the crossing loops which were eventually provided at all stations except Wartle, Plaidy and Banff Bridge. The longest single line stretch was thus the 7½ miles between the junction and Rothienorman.

However, services on the branch were never particularly heavy. In 1863, still in the days of the nominally independent local company, the GNSR provided four trains each way, variously designated mixed, parliamentary etc, as on the Oldmeldrum line. Fares were one (old) penny per mile for parliamentary class passengers, one penny farthing for third class and twopence for first class. Initially this service was entirely self-contained to the branch, though later through trains or coaches ran to and from Aberdeen. The service was based at 'Macduff' with a first up train at 6.50 followed by three others at 10am, 12.40 and 6.10pm. These returned from Inveramsay at 9.20am, 2.28, 5.48 and 8.18pm respectively. Times over the branch varied between 92 and 105 minutes, presumably depending on the amount of goods traffic to be handled. An engine shed and turntable were provided at the original terminus. When the line was extended in 1872, the substantial stone shed and turntable were situated on the up side of

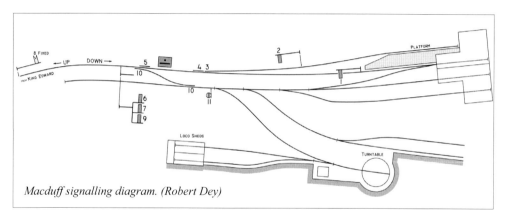

Macduff signalling diagram. (Robert Dey)

the line. However, there were a couple of crossings at Turriff, so some of the service must have been supplied from the facilities at Inveramsay. Extra sidings were put in at Turriff in 1868, in response to the developing traffic.

Once again some light is thrown on that traffic by the Great North's statistics issued in 1871 to cover the year 1869-1870. These reveal that the Macduff line was earning £114 per annum per mile, second bottom above the lowly Strathspey line. The Macduff branch's revenue amounted to about £14,000 which, with expenses being under £10,000, gave an annual profit of some £4,500 to the line. That represented a return on capital of 1.29% if traffic to or from the main line is excluded, 4.25% if it is included. Consequently the Macduff line was providing significant returns for the GNSR as a whole, and presumably there would have been a further improvement once the railway was opened to Macduff proper in 1872.

One of the groups to benefit were the fisher folk of the Banffshire coast. From 1863 the local fishwives could get day return tickets at single fare and a half from Banff & Macduff to all stations along the branch, with the exception of Wartle; perhaps its inhabitants were too few to attract the fishwives, or they were not fish lovers. Also, from the 1880s, the fisher 'lasses' who gutted fish in the east coast ports could get cheap tickets to their destinations in East

King Edward looking north on 6th October 1954. The loop, signal box and footbridge have all disappeared but there is still some traffic in the goods yard. (J L Stevenson)

Banff Bridge in June 1949, when repainting appears to have been in progress. Two years later, the clutter had gone and the poster boards were in position on the station. The building was later converted into a house and still serves that purpose.   *(J L Stevenson)*

Anglia and elsewhere. By that time too fresh Banffshire fish could be sent by rail to the great cities of the south, as well as more local destinations. Others to benefit financially from the railway were the parishes through which the line passed. For instance in 1865 in the parish of Turriff the Banff, Macduff & Turriff Extension Railway was rated at £192 per annum, and the Aberdeen & Turriff at £699; which obligations the GNSR of course took over in the following year.

Once into the 1870s the Great North began to build up traffic. Nor were its 'customers' forgotten. For instance the rather mean station at Banff Bridge, which had been the focus of a number of complaints, was extended by the addition of two waiting rooms. According the *Banffshire Journal* in September, 1877, this provided 'comfortable shelter' to the no doubt grateful users. However, the Great North in the 1870s was still recovering from the financial strictures of its earlier days and it was to be the 1880s and 1890s before significant improvements in services and facilities were offered to its customers. In 1880 Mr Moffatt, the new general manager of the GNSR, proposed and effected a new return trip from Macduff to Aberdeen in the morning and back in the afternoon; the stock would spend the night in Macduff yard not the shed.

The earlier part of the 1880s was marred by a terrible accident at Inverythan between Auchterless and Fyvie in 1882, which will be detailed in chapter 6. By then there had been changes in the passenger services. There were still four mixed trains each way on the branch, leaving Macduff at 6, 8.40am, 12.15 and 4pm; and returning from Inveramsay at 8.08am, 12.05, 2.20 and 6.10pm. Timings on the whole were quicker than in the 1860s; there were still no through services to the main line, though connections at Inveramsay were generally reasonable. The evening 'path' on the branch was now occupied by a 'special goods' which took only 90 minutes each way over the whole branch; presumably it was carrying perishable traffic. By August, 1887, *Bradshaw* was advertising the same four mixed trains each way on weekdays at much the same times. However, on Saturday evenings the goods was replaced by a return trip for passengers departing Macduff at 6.20 and Inveramsay at 8.50pm, which provided a later connection from Aberdeen.

While we shall again be looking at staff later, files from the 1880s reveal that the station master, or 'agent' in Great North parlance, at Plaidy in the early part of that decade was Mr James Minto, before he was transferred to the bigger – ie with two platforms – station at Auchterless. He seems to have decided that the less the folks in the Aberdeen headquarters knew about what was going on in the more remote parts of the county the better for all concerned. Hence he was in receipt of various complaints about his paperwork, but unfortunately his replies seem not to have survived.

By the 1890s the Great North was becoming more prosperous under Mr Moffatt's managership, and the Macduff branch by December 1895 had five return trips per day, with times on the branch varying between 62 and 80 minutes, depending on crossing times and any goods shunting required. Through times to Aberdeen had not really improved, about two hours being the best. However, the races to the north in that year had got the mail into Aberdeen earlier. A postal train connected with the mails from the south and dropped a van at Inveramsay, to be taken on to Macduff by the first down train.

There was some excitement on the line in the mid 1890s. In the first week of 1895 the Macduff branch was badly snowed up for some days. Then early on 11th September 1895 in a fierce storm the Turriff booking office was struck by lightning, which damaged the telegraph instrument and started a small fire; this was, however, soon put out by the station staff who had been alerted. Oddly enough a similar strike in 1932 burned Inveramsay station to the ground. Fyvie was to get its share of excitement in 1896 when the King and Queen of Spain stayed for a few days with Lord Leith at Fyvie castle, arriving and departing by train at Fyvie station.

Apart from repairing Turriff station, the Great North were much engaged at this time in

MACDUFF FROM THE WEST.

The view from the Hill of Doune, just to the west of Macduff, shows how the station was built on a site above the sea. The locomotive shed is on the right with the overall roof of the stone station building in the distance. Access to the town was via the road in the middle, either downhill or uphill via the church. Most of the town is hidden behind the church on the skyeline. (GNSRA collection)

effecting improvements to the line and its stations. 1892 saw the building of two new signal boxes at Auchterless, North and South, both gabled timber boxes GNSR type 2b. In 1895 King Edward got another of the 2b design when the loop was opened, while in the same year Macduff got a box unlike any other type: a wooden building of vertical boards with a hipped roof. At the same time 'telephonic communication' was installed at Macduff station and at Banff (Harbour). Then in 1900 Turriff got a new box of type 3a design: a hipped roof erection, but with horizontal boarding.

Also in the 1890s there was interest in proposed lines extending from various stations on the Macduff branch. The first proposal came in 1893 when there were ideas of joining the Macduff and Fraserburgh lines. Various routes and termini were proposed, but the 'core' line was to serve the villages of Cuminestown, Garmond, New Byth and New Deer; in these places the populations were all reckoned in the hundreds rather than the thousands. Nothing came of the proposals at that point. However, in about 1895, just before the passing of the Light Railways Act of 1896, the proposals were resurrected. The villages served were to be the same as before and the preferred termini were to be Turriff and Maud. This time the line would extend to fifteen miles and cost £90,000. Under the proposed new legislation government and local authority grants would be allowed. There was some criticism at a meeting in Cuminestown of the Great North's efforts to serve the area; though its support would almost certainly been necessary to build and operate this 'Central Buchan' line. In the event nothing more was heard of the Central Buchan proposal as such.

To move forward some years after the above legislation was passed: interest was revived in that area in the new century, when a narrow gauge line, called the West Buchan Light Railway, was proposed between Turriff and Maud or Brucklay. It would serve the same villages as the Central Buchan, plus New Pitsligo. The gauge was initially to be two feet six inches, then three feet. Others deemed standard gauge more sensible, as the Great North would be the probable operators of the line. The actual promoters of the line were the Scottish Light Railways and

The goods yard at Macduff was still quite busy in 1954. The turntable was in regular use so that locomotives facing the stiff climb up the hill could run chimney first.   *(J L Stevenson)*

The interior of Macduff station cannot have been very attractive to potential passengers although some of the comforts such as seats would have been removed by 1954 when this photograph was taken. Doors on the left led to the booking office and waiting room. *(J L Stevenson)*

Development Syndicate, not the GNSR, though the latter indicated its willingness to operate the line. Coal, peat and stone would be carried, as well as 20,000 passengers per annum, the latter in tramway type coaches. Stations would be of the simplest design and electric traction was talked about. There were the necessary negotiations with the Treasury, the Board of Agriculture for Scotland and the Light Railway Commissioners about building and financing the line. Proceedings were slow, and the outbreak of war in 1914 put a stop to them. They were revived after 1918, but again unsuccessfully.

Meanwhile in April, 1896, there had been proposals for a light railway from Rothienorman to Tillynaught, the junction for the Banff branch, with the people of Aberchirder seeking support from the Great North. The latter was prepared to back the line, if the local people were prepared to give some positive support. This scheme, under the title of Aberdeenshire Light Railways, was tied in with one for a line between Aberdeen and Echt and possibly one from Ballater to Braemar; and indeed it did reach the stage of an application being made to the Light Railway Commissioners. In 1897 there were various changes of plan, and letters pro and con in the press, particularly with regard to the Echt line. The Rothienorman to Tillynaught scheme seems to have got lost in all this; neither was the Echt line built. The Great North was probably glad to see the back of all these, probably unremunerative, schemes as it faced the new century.

Into the Twentieth Century

By the first year of that new century the timetable showed five trains each way on the Macduff line plus a Saturday evening service. Also there were now through carriages between Aberdeen and the branch on most trains. There were also various special excursions as in the summer of 1901, when a special train carried 250 – 300 Free Gardeners and Oddfellows on a visit from Turriff to Glasgow.

1903 again saw a statistical survey of the GNSR system for the year to 31st July of that

Macduff in the 1930s. The stock in the bay platform includes two North British designed covered fish vans which could be run at speed.   (LGRP)

year. Passenger journeys on the branch were over 207,000, bringing in £8,192. The 3,189 trucks of livestock and 57,596 tons of goods and minerals brought in £9,438; giving a grand total of £17,630. There were no detailed expenditure figures given for the branch, but overall it came to about £9,000. This gave a reasonable profitability of 16.7d per train mile and an operating ratio of 57.75%; the third best after the Lossiemouth and Alford Branches. The branches were in the same order as regards return on investment, the Macduff line coming in at 2.95%, some way behind the first two.

However, coal consumption on the branch was 65lbs per mile, the highest on the GNSR system, where the average was 45lbs. Since there is no reason to believe that Macduff line enginemen were particularly profligate in this respect, the figure must be a reflection of the heavier gradients on the branch, compared with say its neighbour the Banff branch, where only 29 lbs per mile were consumed. Macduff line enginemen totalled three drivers and four firemen, with an extra of each during the summer season. The former received between 4/6 and 6/6 per day, while the latter got 3/- to 3/10; multiply by six to get their weekly wages. Of traffic staff there were on the Macduff line nine station agents, nine clerks, twelve porters, six signalmen, two guards and two others. That probably works out at one agent and one clerk at each of the nine stations on the branch; this may have represented the total staff complement at Wartle, Plaidy and Banff Bridge stations, with the porters and signalmen shared out among the other six. It was noted that the highest paid signalman was that at Macduff, who received £52/17/6 per annum, with his other signalling colleagues receiving a few pounds less. Station agents averaged £65 per annum, with clerks earning about half of that.

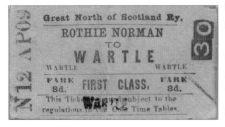

The fact that Wartle, Plaidy and Banff Bridge were regarded as lesser establishments is emphasised in the RCH *Handbook of Stations* for 1904. While Fyvie, Turriff and Macduff offered facilities for all six RCH categories of traffic,

Rothienorman did not offer facilities for furniture vans, and Wartle, Auchterless, Plaidy and King Edward did not accept carriages by passenger train either. Banff Bridge was solely a passenger station. Cranes of 1 ton 5 cwts lift were available at Rothienorman, Fyvie, Auchterless, Turriff and Macduff; the rest had none.

A facility at Turriff station not shown in the RCH *Handbook* was its automatic picture postcard vending machine. This

London & North Eastern Railway.

LUGGAGE.

Auchterless

From ....

was a 1905 invention of porter Alex Taylor, which dispensed postcards showing local views, presumably including Turriff station, when the customer put an old penny in the slot. No doubt Mr Taylor also spent part of his time in dealing with that other station facility where one could also spend a penny!

About this time the Great North was giving its attention to instituting motor bus services to settlements in its area not directly served by rail services. The first started between Ballater and Braemar in 1904, but it was thought wise to seek parliamentary authority in 1906, and from then on various schemes were initiated throughout Great North territory. None of these connected directly with stations on the Macduff branch, but Aberchirder was served by bus from Huntly, which no doubt finally put paid to the earlier proposals for a light railway from Rothienorman through Aberchirder to Tillynaught. However, GNSR timetables, both public and working,

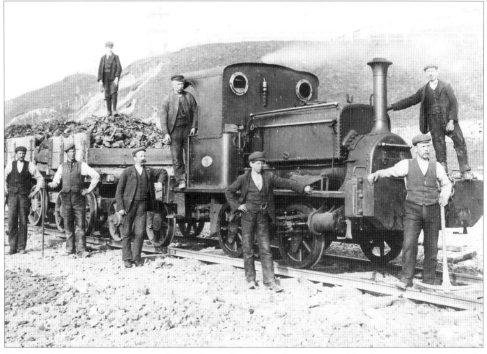

The Macduff line was never extended to the harbour but a loco was used by the contractor during the improvement works in the early 1900s. Built by Manning Wardle, it had been used on the construction of the line from Alnwick to Cornhill before coming north. It was advertised for sale in 1907, but appears to have found no takers.　　　　　　　　　　　　　　　　　　　　　　　*(Banffshire Journal)*

Macduff line timetable for July 1911. The empty carriages of the 6.45pm Wednesdays train from Macduff returned by the 6.10pm down goods. Livestock trucks could be attached to passenger trains on Tuesdays and Thursdays of Turriff sales.

also showed coach services 'not controlled by the Company, but announced by Owners to run in connection with Trains'. These included a coach service between Maud and Turriff along the line of the proposed Buchan Central Railway. One coach each way daily, which in fact did not connect particularly closely with trains, hardly suggests that a railway along the route would have been notably successful.

The timetable for 1911 is illustrated on the right. By 1914, the milk train ran on Sunday afternoon. For the first two years of the war there was little diminution of services, but by 1916 there was some thinning out. The government wanted the railways to economise on scarce fuel, so fewer trains were run. Moreover railway companies were having to economise on manpower. For, although railway employees were generally in a 'reserved' category not liable to summary conscription, in fact many of them did serve in the forces. In all, 609 members of staff served, 22% of the total, and 93 names are recorded on the Company's War Memorial in Aberdeen station.

TO MACDUFF—DOWN TRAINS.

Miles.	STATIONS.	1 Mon only Eng. only.	2 Gds.	3 Pass. and Mail.	4 Pass.	5 Pass.	6 Pass.	7 Goods	8 Pass	9 Sats only Pass.	
		a.m.	a.m.	a.m.	a m.	p.m.	p.m.	p.m.	p.m.	p.m.	
	Aberdeen de	.....	4 0	8 5	10 5	1 20	3 55	2 0	5 45	7 45	....
	Keith	.....	1 45	6 20	8 40	1 3	3*33	12 20	5 30	7 0	....
	Inveramsay de	1 22	6 33	8 43	10 45	2 25	4 47	6 10	6 50	8 45	....
3¾	Wartle	.....	6 50	8 51	10 53	2 34	4 55	6 26	6 58	8 53	....
7½	Rothie-Nor.	.....	7 10	8 59	11 1	2 43	5 3	6 44	7 7	9 1	....
10¾	Fyvie	1 47	7 27	9 7	11 8	2 51	5 10	7 0	7 15	9 8	....
14	Auchterless ar	Stop.	....	.....	.....	....	....	7 9	....	.....	....
..	Do. de	.....	7 39	9 14	11 14	2 59	5 16	7 33	7 22	9 14	....
18	Turriff ar	.....	7 49	.....	.....	....	....	7 43	....	....	....
..	Do. de	.....	7 58	9 23	11 23	3 10	5 25	7 53	7 32	9 23	....
22½	Plaidy	.....	8 12	9 32	11 32	3 20	5 34	8 7	7 41	9 32	....
24¾	King-Edward	.....	8 21	9 38	11 38	3 27	5 40	8 16	7 47	9 38	....
29½	Banff Bridge	.....	....	9 47	11 47	3 37	5 49	.....	7 57	9 47	....
29¾	Macduff ar	.....	8 33	9 50	11 50	3 40	5 52	8 28	8 0	9 50	....

FROM MACDUFF—UP TRAINS.

Miles.	STATIONS.	1 Mon only Milk.	2 Pass	3 Pass.	4 Goods	5 Pass. b	6 Pass and Mail	7 G'ds	8 Pass.	9 Wed only Pass.	10 Sats only Pass.
		a.m.	a.m.	a.m	a.m.	p.m.	p.m.	p.m.	p.m.	p.m.	p.m.
..	Macduff de.	.....	6 20	8 40	9 20	1 0	3 15	3 40	5 0	6 45	6 45
¼	Banff Bridge	.....	6 22	8 42	.....	1 2	3 17	....	5 2	6 47	6 47
5	King-Edward	.....	6 32	8 52	9†42	1 12	3 27	3 54	5 12	6 57	6 57
7¼	Plaidy	.....	6 37	8 57	9 51	1 17	3 32	4 8	5 17	7 2	7 2
11¾	Turriff ar	.....	....	.....	10 2	....	....	....	....	7 10	.....
..	Do. de.	.....	6 46	9 [illegible]	10 13	1 26	3 41	4 23	5 26	Stop.	7 12
15¾	Auchterless	.....	6 54	9 14	10 28	1 34	3 49	4 36	5 34	.....	7 22
19	Fyvie	1 52	7 1	9 21	10 47	1 41	3 56	4 50	5 41	.....	7 30
22¼	Rothie ar.	.....	....	.....	10 59	....	....	5 1	....	....	.....
..	Do. dep.	.....	7 10	9 30	11 15	1 49	4 4	5 15	5 49	.....	7 38
26	Wartle	2 11	7 19	9 39	11 30	1 57	4 12	5 30	5 57	.....	7 47
29¾	Inveramsay ar	2 17	7 26	9 46	11 40	2 3	4 18	5 40	6 3	.....	7 54
	Aberdeen	3 47	8 30	10 55	2p17	3 0	5 10	6 45	7 0	.....	8 52
	Keith	.....	9 8	12 0	6 40	3*49	5 35	....	8*17	.....	.....

TURRIFF SALE ON TUESDAYS AND THURSDAYS.—10·45 a.m. and 2·25 p.m. Trains may lift on rear of Passenger portion a Truck of Live Stock from Turriff to Macduff; and 8·40 a.m. Train may lift on rear a Truck of Live Stock from King-Edward to Turriff.

* Keith Town. † Due to arrive King-Edward at 9·32 a.m.

b Passengers for Insch and beyond are to travel to Inverurie by 1·3 p.m. Up Train, without extra charge, to join 2·20 p.m. Down Express Train, except on Saturdays, when they will be taken forward from Inveramsay by 1·37 p.m. Down Train.

Macduff line timetable for summer 1911.

Owing to the war the Great North was required to transport large quantities of timber so necessary for the war effort. Though most of this came over the Speyside and Deeside lines, the whole GNSR system was involved in this effort. Barclay-Harvey (p218) notes that the herring traffic also increased hugely during the war, because the north east ports were closed to all but essential traffic and the export markets had been lost. There was also the threat from enemy warships operating in the area. Consequently more traffic had to travel via inland routes, and for long distance traffic that still meant rail. It is known that there was an increase in herring carryings on the Great North of over 46,000 tons per annum and the increase in general traffic may have been about the same. There are no details, but no doubt the Macduff branch carried its share of all this. Oddly enough, although Macduff was very much a fishing port, there is little mention of fish traffic in the branch working timetables but trains were run specifically for livestock and milk. Vans carrying fish could be attached to passenger, mixed or 'special goods' trains.

The staff at Macduff in late GNSR days. (GNSRA collection)

There was indeed a special train on 11th October, 1918, one month before the end of the war. Moreover it involved a special platform being built for one day's use only. This was at Rothiebrisbane Farm, about one mile south of Fyvie station. The occasion was a sale of shorthorn cattle, one of five held that week at various locations, including Aberdeen and Oldmeldrum. The Great North *Review* (No.115 p363) shows that the platform was probably south of the farm close to an overbridge carrying a farm road. This platform must have been short, as the special train of six coaches had to draw forward one or more times to let passengers on or off; they had to book tickets for Fyvie. This train had departed from Aberdeen at 9.30am and reached Rothiebrisbane at 10.40, before going on to Fyvie. Passengers left Rothiebrisbane at 3.45pm before reaching Aberdeen at 5.07. Thus the 'station', presumably of timber, had been open for five hours and five minutes. It was not unknown for railway companies to erect temporary stations for special events, but the above 'temporariness' must be exceptional. The sale of 68 cattle raised £17,667, but there is no record of any special train for them.

After the war passenger services on the branch returned to more or less normal, though matters were not helped by a rail strike in 1920. By the time of the final GNSR working timetable of October, 1922, there were three passenger and two mixed trains daily over the whole Macduff line. The reintroduction of mixed trains had allowed the goods services to be reduced from two to one return trip daily. The Saturday evening return trip had ceased although the Sundays only milk train to Turriff had survived. Typical timings over the branch were 65-70 minutes for passenger trains and 95-100 for mixed. This timetable showed only a relatively small reduction from the pre-war services, but already troubles were looming as first local bus operators, then bigger combines like Alexander's, put direct services to Aberdeen on the A947 road, which paralleled the railway from Fyvie northwards. However, that was to be a matter for the new LNER to deal with.

Tillynaught was always a junction, opening with the line in 1859, but originally it had a simple layout with one siding and platform faces on both the Banff and Portsoy lines. This changed in 1884 when the line was extended westward from Portsoy as part of the new through route to Elgin. Tillynaught was rebuilt with a passing place on the main line and a separate platform and run-round loop for the trains which shuttled to and from Banff. This view from the south end shows 4-4-0 No.62262 on a train which has arrived from Banff in July 1954. In the early days there was a turntable at Banff but there was never one at Tillynaught, so locos had to work tender first to Banff.   *(Graham Maxtone collection)*

Ladysbridge looking over the valley to the Banffshire District Lunatic Asylum, one of many established around the country in Victorian Britain. The locomotive is a rebuilt Cowan 2-4-0. The photograph can be dated between 1880, when the first of these locomotives was rebuilt, and 1888 when signalling was installed. Ladysbridge was the main intermediate station on the branch.   *(R D Drummond/GNSRA)*

Chapter 4

Banff Branch until 1922

In this chapter, when I refer to the Banff branch, the line from Tillynaught to Banff (Harbour) station is intended, unless otherwise noted; the 'Harbour' suffix was dropped in 1928. Indeed for most of its life the Banff branch was just that, an adjunct to the main line running from Keith and Grange along the Moray Firth coast to Elgin. However, in its early history it was in effect the main line of the Banffshire Railway, and this latter concern must be given some consideration.

All of the six miles of the Banff branch, apart from a short distance at Tillynaught Junction, were in the parishes of Banff and Boyndie. Banff and Boyndie had been one parish until their separation in 1635. The name Boyndie probably comes from a Gaelic word meaning a stream. The main settlement in the parish was, and is, Whitehills, a fishing port noted in 1840 for its haddock. The population of the parish in 1831 had been 1,501. An annual fair was held at Ordens, and timber was also important in the parish. In 1921 seine netting was introduced to Whitehills, and by 1951 the population was 1,872. Aberdeen-Angus cattle were reared in the parish along with sheep, poultry and pigs. Whitehills was about 1½ miles from Ladysbridge station; just about within walking distance. Ladysbridge Mental Hospital was opened in 1860, just after the railway, and closed in 2003. Doubtless it provided traffic for Ladysbridge station, but the *Third Statistical Account* noted of the branch line: 'Passenger traffic is light, however, as the bus, with its hourly service in winter and half-hourly in summer, is more convenient and a cheaper mode of travel.'

The 1836 *New Statistical Account* derives the name Banff from the Gaelic word for a stream, possibly the Burn of Boyne. However, various alternative explanations, such as Banff coming from a word for pigs, can be found in *The Book of Banff* (p12). Banff possibly became a royal burgh around 1190, and certainly by 1372, when it was the county town of Banffshire. As such it suffered much damage in the Civil War and the two Jacobite rebellions. Another famous event, celebrated in song, was the execution at Banff in 1700 of James Macpherson, hero or brigand, depending on whom you believe. The burgh's population in 1831 had been 2,935, with 776 in the landward part of the parish. At that time the main livestock reared were crossbred cattle, with few sheep. Much grain was produced and the salmon fishery on the River Deveron was abundant; lobsters and other shellfish were also sent to London by sea. The herring fishery was also very important. There were breweries and a distillery nearby, and Messrs Fraser's foundry 'executed all kinds of metal work'. Coals for these concerns and for domestic use were imported by sea from Sunderland, while there were daily stages to both Aberdeen and Inverness via the turnpike road, and also to Peterhead.

The writer of the preamble to the *Third Statistical Account on the County of Banff* notes that the railway carried much timber south during World War 1. However, after the Grouping slow progress on the updating of track, signals, etc, played into the hands of motorised traffic. Passenger numbers fell severely, and there was an increasing effect on freight; cheap fares etc came too late. During World War 2 petrol rationing led to much increased traffic on the railways, but thereafter renewed road competition led to the closure of some branches. In all, a very perceptive survey of the LNER years, to which we shall return later.

The *Third Statistical Account* on Banff itself notes that its population in the 1951 census had been 3,357, plus 534 in the rural area of the parish. Livestock raised was mainly cattle and pigs, with increasing numbers of poultry. Again much grain was produced, along with turnips and potatoes. However shipping had virtually disappeared from Banff harbour, apart from the occasional collier. No fish, either herring or white fish, was landed at Banff, though Whitehills was still a fishing port. The distillery, relocated in 1853, and the foundry were still in production. Brief mention is made of the still operating Banff branch, and the withdrawal of trains at Banff Bridge is noted; as is a 'good service of buses' to Aberdeen, Elgin, Fraserburgh and other parts. These would have been of use to the increasing numbers of holiday makers to the Banff area.

Therefore there was much in the Banff area to interest the railway promoters of the 1840s. Consideration is now turned to how a Banffshire railway came to fruition.

The Banffshire Railway

As we have seen above, Banff was an early target for railway promoters. The original act of 1846 for the GNSR had included a branch from Grange to Banff, but the Great North's financial problems in getting even its main line built precluded it from proceeding with any of the proposed branches.

However, once the Great North's main line had been completed to Keith, local interest in a line to Banff again surfaced. The proposal was still for a line from Grange to Banff, with a branch from Tillynaught west to Portsoy, another fishing port; as is indicated in the title of the company: the Banff, Portsoy & Strathisla Railway – Keith is the main town in Strathisla. Its bill

The Banffshire Railway crossed roads on the level in three places. This is Inverboyndie, not far from Banff.   *(Graham Maxtone collection)*

became an act on 17th July, 1857 (20&21 Victoria c53), and authorised a capital of £90,000 in £10 shares, with the usual borrowing powers of one third of that. The contractor was to be B.&E. Blyth of Edinburgh at a price of £62,300, of which the Blyths would receive £12,500 in shares of the company. Their resident engineer was to be William Keir, who remained as engineer to the local company until the Great North took over the working of the line in 1863. Other offices were held by two local men, John Forbes as secretary and James Grierson as general manager; the latter to be succeeded in 1859 by George Morrison. The members of the board were also mainly local men, the chairman being T.C. Bruce, factor of the Earl of Seafield, one of the main landowners in the area.

This last appointment was to be of importance in the history of the company, for Seafield, and more particularly Bruce, were also very much involved in the Inverness & Aberdeen Junction Railway, later a constituent of the Highland Railway, which had proceeded as far east as Keith and prevented the Great North from building its main line all the way to Inverness as it had originally intended. Had the I&AJR managed to push its way to Banff and the coast over the new branch line, it would have been a matter of great concern to the Great North, who were thus most interested in the BP&SR.

Initially only £40,200 worth of shares were sold, but arrangements were made for the line to be built, in the first place as far as Tillynaught, then to Durn Toll Bar somewhat short of Portsoy, and to Hill of Boyndie a similar distance short of Banff, where the level crossing of that name was later to be situated. Three contracts replacing the original one were now made. There was some grumbling in Banff when it was decided to advance the Portsoy line to the south eastern edge of that town, and to assuage feelings in Banff its branch was to be extended to approximately where the later Golf Club House halt was situated. However, extension to Banff harbour, on the northern side of the town, was later agreed. All these manoeuvrings resulted in the main line to Banff being sixteen miles long, though the stretch from Tillynaught was only six miles, while the branch to Portsoy was three and a quarter miles.

Despite the financial problems and the consequent wrangling, construction started in 1858 and proceeded reasonably well over the relatively level ground. Though there had been earlier proposals for the Great North to work the line, by January, 1859, negotiations were going on with Blyth to procure two locomotives, and in March to purchase two composite and two third class carriages; later thirty goods wagons and a brake van were obtained. By July the traffic manager, Mr Grierson, was in post, and at Banff there were to be a station master, porter, ticket boy, clerk, engine driver, fireman and cleaner; level crossing keepers were appointed for Mill of Boyndie, Ladysbridge and Blairshinnoch. Fares were set at GNSR rates of twopence per mile for first class, one penny farthing for third class and one penny for 'parliamentary' or 'government' class. By the opening day the company was overdrawn by £7,240 in addition to the authorised overdraft of £15,000. The Company then exercised its borrowing powers and obtained £28,000 by way of debentures.

On the opening day, Saturday 30th July, 1859, services were only to run to the temporary termini, but the festivities were literally brought to an abrupt halt when the first train was derailed on faulty track about four miles north of Grange; it was two days before proper services began. Excessive speed over the dubious track is also thought to have been a factor in the fiasco. Only one locomotive had been delivered and another was hired, perhaps significantly, from the I&AJR. Under such strictures the service was operated Grange – Tillynaught – Portsoy – Tillynaught – Banff, and vice versa. By October another locomotive had arrived and the service ran from Grange direct to Banff, with a shuttle service in connection from Tillynaught

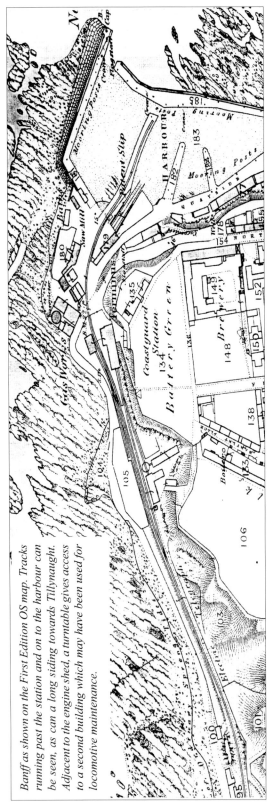

Banff as shown on the First Edition OS map. Tracks running past the station and on to the harbour can be seen, as can a long siding towards Tillynaught. Adjacent to the engine shed, a turntable gives access to a second building which may have been used for locomotive maintenance.

to Portsoy; there were through coaches between Banff and Portsoy. Also in October the gatekeeper at Ladysbridge received a pay increase as he was now also acting as station master. Ladysbridge opened as a station on 1st October along with the platform at Ordens. The latter was not always shown in the timetables; it disappeared for periods of several years, but it is quite possible that trains called when passengers presented themselves.

By 31st March, 1860, the line had been extended to the intended terminus at Banff Harbour, but only for freight. The first train, of eleven wagons and a carriage carrying the directors, was hauled by a locomotive decked with a masonic flag and evergreens, and was cheered into the station by crowds on both sides of the line. Passenger services began on 1st May.

While the extension to serve Banff harbour proper had been authorised with the line, it of course could not be opened until after the passenger station at Banff was opened in 1860. In any case by 1868 the Great North, by then the owner of the line, gave notice on 14th May that it would cease to work the harbour extension. Perhaps traffic coming to the harbour by sea had fallen off due to the railway bringing goods more quickly from the south. So the extension had a short career, probably of little use, and along with the similar history of the Portsoy harbour line, may have turned the Great North against a line to the harbour at Macduff.

The initial service between Grange and Banff was three trains each way; this continued when the Portsoy line was run as a separate branch. In 1863 trains departed Banff at 9.15 (mixed) to Grange, 10.15am to Portsoy, 12.20 to Grange, with through carriages to Portsoy, and 5pm (mixed) to Grange, with through carriages to Portsoy. The corresponding down trains left Grange for Banff at 10.45am, 2 and 5pm (mixed); these had connections or through carriages at Tillynaught from Portsoy, which also had a through mixed train to Banff at 9.27am. Trains took just over one hour from Grange to Banff, though one took only 45 minutes for a time. All trains had first, third and parliamentary class accommodation. Such a service would require locomotives to be based at Banff and Portsoy, where there were sheds and turntables.

By 1863, however, the BP&SR was struggling. In its first year it had an income of £5,220 as against expenditure of £3,012, but most of its surplus went on servicing its debts, a scenario familiar to the other lines described in this book. While for the first year of service the maintenance had been carried out, as was common practice, by the contractor, thereafter it became the responsibility of the company. The opening of the Macduff and Turriff route in 1860 gave a more direct route to Aberdeen and would have an adverse effect on the BP&SR's finances. Nevertheless, revenue rose with expenditure, and a dividend of 2% was paid for the half year to February, 1861. There were also problems with staff. Mr Grierson had to be replaced by Mr Morrison, and the first locomotive superintendent, Mr Blackwood, went in October, 1860. His replacement, William Thomson from the GNSR, lasted only one month and was followed by Mr Jeffrey from the I&AJR.

By 1862 there had been thoughts of extending the line west of Portsoy and along the coast towards Elgin. The BP&SR was to promote this, but the Great North would subscribe most of the cost of the extension, which it would work along with the BP&SR. The Great North actually took over the working of the latter, for 60% of receipts, in February, 1863, in advance of the Banffshire Railway Act of 21st July (26&27 Victoria c170). In fact because of financial difficulties the extension beyond Portsoy was not proceeded with at that time, but the name change to the Banffshire Railway became effective immediately.

This Banffshire company, being no longer responsible for working its own line, had little left to do. Indeed it tried to sell surplus BP&SR stationery to the Great North, but the latter was not interested in acquiring notepaper superscribed with the name of a dormant company! The Great North, burdened with the financial problems of supporting nominally independent

The only major structure on the Banff branch was the bridge over the Boyndie Burn. The distillery can be seen in the distance. *(J L Stevenson)*

companies, was eager to absorb these lines fully. The Banffshire had shown its willingness for that to happen in 1865, but was not included in the amalgamations which took in the Oldmeldrum and Macduff companies in 1866; possibly this was because the Banffshire had originally been an independent line operating its own traffic. However, the Great North's Act of 30th July, 1866, in addition to authorising the initial amalgamations and abandoning the extension along the coast, did pave the way for the absorption of the Banffshire company. That took place under the Act of 12th August, 1867 (30&31 Victoria c190), but with retrospective effect from 1st August. All this of course had the effect of debarring the Highland Railway, successors to the I&AJR, from access to the Banff area.

The Banff Branch 1867-1922

While it was to be almost another two decades before the line along the coast was opened in stages, we shall now regard the Banff line simply as a branch from Tillynaught, generally worked like any other GNSR branch. Acworth, in his *Railways of Scotland* of 1889, was to describe the Banff area as one of the most 'prosperous' in Britain, and ports such as Banff among the most 'contented'. So how did the Great North help to bring that about?

The line from Tillynaught to Banff was six miles long and single throughout. In 1867 there was one intermediate station, Ladysbridge at 3½ miles from the junction. Sometimes known as Lady's Bridge, it was situated close to the bridge over the Burn of Boyndie used by Lady Banff on her various journeys; hence the name of the locality. Though the land along the coast was relatively flat, there was a gradual descent from Tillynaught, at 180 feet above sea level, through Ladysbridge at 80 feet to Banff at 22. There were stretches at 1 in 80 for about half a mile through Ordens Platform and for a similar distance a little to the east. The relatively level ground meant that there were the three level crossings mentioned above. The aforementioned Ordens had a somewhat obscure history. It seems to have been a conditional stop in the early timetables – in 1860 it is mentioned as 'sidings' – but it disappeared from the 1864 timetable.

A short siding was provided for Inverboyndie Distillery, seen here in October 1954. Traffic was worked to and from this siding by a separate working from Banff.   *(J L Stevenson)*

Ladysbridge from the west end on 4th October 1954, when there was still some traffic in the goods yard. The level crossing is beyond the station building. (J L Stevenson)

Quick thinks it may have continued in conditional and/or private use, at least intermittently. It appears as a passengers only station in the 1904 RCH *Handbook of Stations*, before it was again publicly advertised during World War 1.

Once again the GNSR provides us with a picture of the line as it entered the 1870s with its statistical summaries for 1869-1870. At that time the ex-Banffshire railway was earning £166 per mile per annum, the third best performing branch, though it was a long way behind the Buchan and Lossiemouth lines. Total revenue was about £8,000, while expenses came to about £4,500, leaving a profit of £3,500. That represented about 2.5% on capital, if main line traffic is excluded, and 5.25%, if it is included; which was near the average for all branches.

The *Banffshire Journal* in January, 1878, reported a curious incident where a parcel from London, addressed to Banff Bridge station, was misdirected to Banff Harbour station. While that is perhaps understandable in itself, the sequel is less so. Instead of the parcel being given to a porter to take on foot over a distance of about thirty minutes walking, it was consigned by rail via Grange and Inveramsay to Banff Bridge, a total of 74 miles taking about five hours. As the *Journal* remarks: 'No red tapism ever perpetrated in government offices was worse than this mode of dispatch.'

The incident, unimportant in itself, does, however, highlight the question of why Macduff and Banff were not directly linked via a rail bridge parallel to the road bridge over the Deveron: a problem that has occasionally puzzled commentators over the years. A couple of the early plans for lines in this area had proposed just such a connection, but the idea seems to have died with the proposals. Perhaps the fact that the BP&SR/Banffshire was the first railway to get to Banff proper may provide a clue. Aware that its route to Aberdeen was somewhat roundabout and that the Macduff extension was soon to approach that place, the BP&SR would have realised that a connection to the new line would have meant that the latter had a much shorter route, at much cheaper fares – 4/2d as against 5/4d, a saving of 1/2d on a parliamentary single from Banff to Aberdeen – via Turriff to Aberdeen, with a consequent effect on the traffic and revenue of the BP&SR.

On the other hand, should the Turriff and Macduff extension line when it arrived in the area have had ideas of an extension or branch into Banff itself, then it would have been vigorously opposed, again for the above reasons. In addition there would have been problems in selecting the route because of the steeply rising ground on either side of the river. While the bridge may not have been particularly long, it would have been relatively costly, at least as far as the two impoverished local companies were concerned, and possibly not considered a justifiable expense. One is left to wonder how many people actually did trudge from central Banff to Banff Bridge to save themselves 1/2d on a single ticket to Aberdeen. Probably finance as well as railway politics came into the equation. When it took over, the Great North seems not to have bothered about the matter. Telephones were installed at Macduff and Banff Harbour stations in 1895, but it is not clear whether they communicated with each other, or only with their respective branches. Perhaps the Great North regarded that matter in the same way as it did the Boddam branch, where building a sensible extension to Peterhead would have impacted on the traffic and revenue of the older, longer line through Maud.

The December, 1884, working timetable shows trains departing from Banff at 5.15, 8.15, 11.50am, 3.10 and 6.20pm, with returns from Grange at 9.30am, 1.10, 4.35 and 7.30pm. The timetable notes that the 6.20pm from Banff conveyed first and third class and fish, while all the others were mixed. As with the other lines dealt with in this book, the GNSR seems to have been reluctant to run trains dedicated to freight only. That would keep the mileage figures down, and delays to passenger would seem to have been acceptable. Timings over the six miles between Banff and Tillynaught were between fifteen and twenty minutes, so passengers may not have been all that enamoured of the arrangement. There were additional trains from Portsoy arriving in Banff at 8.55am, 12.30 and 3.55pm, and departing at 9.40am and 1.20pm. Some of these had coach connections at Tochieneal for Buckie or Cullen when that was the temporary terminus of the Coast line.

The driver and fireman of class K no.43 look to the photographer at Ladysbridge while working a train to Banff. The first vehicle is a passenger brake van.   *(GNSRA collection)*

The restricted site of Banff station is illustrated in this view from the west end in August 1956. The loco shed is on the right with the main running line in front of it. The goods shed and the one-time extension to the harbour are in the distance. *(John Grant)*

When the Coast line was completed to Elgin in 1886, the service to Banff was increased as it now had to connect with trains in both directions at Tillynaught. In the August, 1887, *Bradshaw* the service was given as eleven trains in each direction. A couple of up trains did not call at Ladysbridge. Timings on the branch were now in the 13 to 20 minutes range. Other traffic was also developing at this time, for in 1888 the dealers Burnett sent a sheep special from Banff with eighteen trucks for destinations on the Highland Railway. Then 26 trucks were sent to Newtonmore on the Highland main line. The empty trucks arrived at Banff at 2.50am and departed full at 5.55. One hopes that the staff were adequately rewarded for this effort on a service which was to become a regular one taking sheep to higher ground for the summer.

By December, 1895, the service was down to ten trains each way; the onset of winter may have dictated the slight decrease in services. While Banff was not yet really regarded as a holiday resort, there would have been some extra summer traffic to the town. Also the inhabitants of the area were keen to get about in summer, for on the annual holiday break in July, 1898, specials were run to Aberdeen and Inverness. The latter, under the sponsorship of the Lodge of Shepherds, attracted over 700 passengers, each paying 3/6 for the return trip in excess of 170 miles. In the same month there was excitement on the branch, when on a circus train between Banff and Buckie there was a disturbance among the animals in one truck which resulted in damage to the vehicle. The train was stopped for a time until running repairs had been completed, then went on its way without further mishap.

The Great North delayed installing interlocked points and signalling for several years, much to the annoyance of the Board of Trade. It was not until 1900 a new signal box, type 2a, was built and signalling installed at Banff. This design of box was constructed until 1888 so it may have come second hand to Banff. It was in the fifth class in the hierarchy of GNSR boxes.

Early in the new century there was further excitement on the branch for in January, 1901, the female crossing keeper at Blairshinnoch (Blairshinnock in some sources) was seriously injured by flying debris when a train demolished the gates closed over the line. The crossing

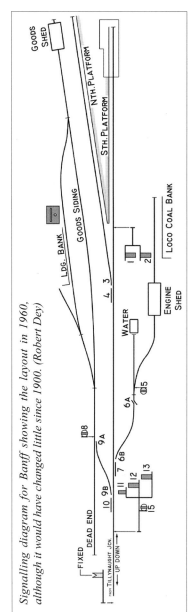

Signalling diagram for Banff showing the layout in 1960, although it would have changed little since 1900. (Robert Dey)

keepers were warned by bells from the nearest signal box when a train was approaching, and it required some judgement to delay road traffic as little as possible while opening the gates in sufficient time for the train to pass. On occasion, as here, misjudgements were made. Another animal caused trouble, this time at Banff station in the next month, when the Fife Arms Hotel horse, which was pulling the mail truck, was frightened by an engine shunting some wagons and started forward. The truck driver was thrown off and injured, but not seriously. Then a note in the weekly circular of 30th May, 1902, states that the turntables at Banff and Portsoy were not to be used; they were only 22ft long so of little use.

The Great North's statistical survey shows that in 1902–1903 the Banff line carried just under 100,000 passengers, who brought in £1,695 of revenue. 333 trucks of livestock and 14,809 tons of general goods and minerals, mainly coal of course, brought in another £1,351 giving total receipts for the branch of just over £3,000. Earnings were about 2.8d per mile, towards the bottom of the list of branches; and the operating ratio was 84.49%, second highest behind Boddam, which gave a return of only 0.98% on investments. The Banff branch figures do not acknowledge the contribution made to main line receipts.

There were fourteen traffic staff altogether on the branch. Station masters were at Banff and Ladysbridge, while clerks would be distributed two and one respectively. There were probably four porters at Banff and one at Ladysbridge; and there was one signalman, one guard and two 'other' staff. In addition the locomotive staff consisted of two drivers and two firemen. Coal consumption was 39lbs per mile, the lowest on the branches, except for Oldmeldrum; coal cost 13/- (65p) per ton. This represented a revenue expenditure of only 15.34d per train mile: the lowest on the branches, perhaps reflecting that the branch was comparatively easy to work.

The 1904 RCH *Handbook of Stations* shows Ladysbridge as handling passengers, goods, livestock and horse boxes, with the help of a two ton crane. Banff in addition could deal with furniture vans and carriages by passenger train. Its crane could lift 2 tons 10cwts. Orden's (sic) Platform, omitted from the *Handbook* in 1890 and 1895, is listed as dealing with passengers but not parcels or miscellaneous traffic; the 1902 working timetable had shown most trains calling there as required. However, it still did not appear in the public timetable. There were no other railway establishments listed for the branch in the 1904 *Handbook*.

The more day to day traffic was listed in the summer 1911 working timetable. This is interesting in that a train carrying goods only left Banff 5.15am, returning from Tillynaught

Golf Club House Halt in October 1954, with Banff in the distance. The original, temporary, terminus was in the middle distance, near where the railway starts to run under the cliff. (J L Stevenson)

at 6.15; it was the only train allowed to take wagons from Ladysbridge to Banff. Thereafter the branch engine was free to deal with the ten return passenger trips on weekdays only. Of these, three up and two down are listed as mixed, and one each way carried mail as well as passengers. Ordens Platform is mentioned as being 'worked in the charge of the guard'. The 9.55am down mixed was to work Boyndie Siding when 'urgently' required, and the 12.23pm down mixed was to call as required. Then the engine would leave Banff at 12.55 and take back any traffic from Boyndie to Banff. The siding was about 1½ miles from Banff and served the distillery which had relocated from Mill of Banff to Inverboyndie in 1863.

However in 1913 the trains on the branch had rather more to do, for on 1st October of that year simple passenger halts were opened at Bridgefoot, 4¾ miles from Tillynaught, and at Golf Club House at 5¼ miles. The first served the small settlement at Inverboyndie, and was slightly closer to Whitehills than Ladysbridge, while the main purpose of the latter halt is obvious. To help passengers, automatic ticket-issuing machines were brought into use at these halts in December 1913. Only a 1d ticket was issued and this was valid to either Banff or Ladysbridge. First class passengers had to purchase two tickets.

These openings occurred while the Great North was embroiled in a court case involving a porter at Tillynaught, William McWilliam. He had joined the GNSR on 3rd April, 1913, and part of his duties involved transferring luggage between main line and Banff branch trains at Tillynaught. On 23rd April he had jumped on to the footboard of a train entering the station from Elgin, presumably to expedite his work, despite that fact that jumping on a moving train was against the company's rules. He had already been warned about doing this, though he claimed to be ignorant of the rule. At any rate he fell from the train and his injuries resulted in the loss of his right leg. In 1914 he brought an action against the Great North, which showed that the accident had occurred during the course of his employment and that the company was thus liable for damages, despite McWilliam breaking the rule. By that time of course the country was on the brink of World War 1, and the Great North had more serious matters to deal with.

As already noted, the first two years of the war brought relatively few changes to the Great North's operations, though since the traffic in both herrings and timber was greatly increased, the Banff branch would have seen its share of that. Fair amounts of herring were still being landed at Banff, and there was much timber in the hinterland of the town. Possibly shortages of staff led to passengers complaining in November, 1916, about names of stations not being called out as trains arrived; a situation not helped by lighting restrictions and drawn blinds. The Great North's answer was to order all trains to call at all stations and halts on the branch; previously they had only called at the halts during daylight hours. At the same time, footwarmers, being in very short supply, were not to be supplied, so passengers on the Banff, and other branches, had to go cold in winter. The notice mentioned Ordens, and it was included in *Bradshaw* from January, 1916, though it had disappeared thence some four years later. Perhaps these dates suggest that there was some increased usage for a reason connected with the war. It was finally admitted permanently to the public timetables by the LNER from July, 1924.

In *Great North Review* (No.116 p381) Major Morrison tells of a holiday spent at Banff about the end of World War 1. He relates how, once the locomotive had drawn its carriages into Banff station and the passengers had disembarked, the engine then shunted the carriages back out, then was uncoupled and ran into its shed; after which the coaches cruised down into the platform by gravity. Young Master Morrison, somewhat against GNSR rules, was allowed to assist the guard in this manoeuvre; a manoeuvre of course rendered necessary by the lack of a proper run round loop at the station. Also in late 1918 there were other visitors to Banff: thirty five members of the band of the Gordon Highlanders. On arrival from Elgin and Cullen in a special reserved coach they gave a concert in Banff, then went on via Macduff to Turriff, where another concert was given before they ended their tour in Aberdeen.

That tour of course indicated that the war was just over and that the Great North could

Ordens looking towards Banff in May 1968, four years after passenger trains ceased. This halt can hardly have changed over the years. The first edition OS map shows a building in the same spot, next to points for a siding on the left.
(Keith Fenwick)

make a start on restoring the pre-war services. The October 1922, working timetable shows that the goods only train had gone, but that there were again ten passenger trains each way on the branch between the 6.50am from Banff and the last arrival there at 8.56pm; three up and two down trains were mixed, but were restricted to drawing a maximum of ten wagons each. Ordens platform, not in the

public timetable at that point, was still to be worked by the guard, while at Bridgefoot and Golf Club House Platform Halts (sic) trains were to call by request. The latter was to be closed from October to April, when at least some of the golfers would be hibernating; though in fact the golfers had largely migrated to the Duff House facility, finally amalgamating with the club there in 1923, and the Golf Club House had become more of a general leisure centre. The 12.25pm mixed from Tillynaught was to drop wagons at Boyndie Siding; the Tillynaught porter was to travel on the train to help in this. Also the 1.35pm mixed from Tillynaught was to lift 'Perishables Traffic and Whisky' from the siding, this time with assistance from a Banff porter. Timings for passenger trains were still about fifteen minutes while mixed ones took twenty.

As on the other branches services had been largely restored to pre-1914 levels, which in general were the best ever, when the LNER was formed. We now turn to look at the operation of the three branch lines in this book under their new owners.

The passenger platforms and overall roof at Banff, with the goods shed on the left in the 1930s. The harbour is in the distance, next to the gasometer. The nearest vehicle in the platform is a Great North passenger brake van. There was a substantial stone building at the other end of the wooden overall roof which included the usual station offices and living accommodation. (LGRP)

Ex-Caledonian Railway 0-4-4 tanks were widely used on branch lines including the Banff branch. No.55185 approaches the terminus on 28th May 1955. This locomotive worked in the area from November 1952 until its withdrawal in June 1961.   *(F W Hampson)*

Macduff in June 1949. On the left, the branch engine is next to the turntable. The lining on the rear of the tender shows that it is still in LNER livery. The train at the platform includes an ex-North Eastern clerestory roofed coach. A few loaded wagons sit in the centre siding ready for the next freight to the south.

(J L Stevenson)

Chapter 5

Grouping, Nationalisation and Closure

Grouping and First Closure

Quite apart from the problems of reorganising several major railway companies into one establishment – with few initial changes in timetables, liveries etc – the LNER soon had to deal with a perennial problem in North East Scotland: snow. In late February and early March, 1924, even the main lines were affected, but the most badly snowed up line was that to Macduff over the exposed uplands of rural Aberdeenshire. It took 77 men from Aberdeen and squads from Macduff, King Edward, Turriff and Fyvie to get the line clear by 7th March.

However, by the late 1920s the LNER was facing what was to become another, and more persistent and perennial problem, which affected all railways: motorised transport in the form of buses and lorries. We have already mentioned that local entrepreneurs had started road transport businesses in the Oldmeldrum and Turriff areas and the same is true of the Banff area in the early 1920s period. Horne's had long run buses, first horse then motor, in the Banff and Macduff areas, and in 1923 the Davidson brothers also started services between the two towns and then a twice weekly service to Aberdeen. There was much rationalisation among bus companies in the late 1920s. Many came together to form the Scottish General (Northern) Omnibus Company in August, 1930, though this was very soon taken over by W. Alexander & Sons. The LNER had of course taken over the GNSR bus services, but in August, 1928, it, along with the other 'Big Four' railway companies, obtained powers to take a stake in the big independent bus companies. They then decided to use these powers extensively rather than operate bus services themselves. Along with the London, Midland & Scottish Railway, they bought a large stake in Alexander's, the idea presumably being that, even if the buses were successful in competition with the railways, the LNER would still have a share in that success.

It is clear from such statistics as are available for the interwar period that local rail services suffered badly at the hands of bus competition. Reductions in passenger numbers between one third and two thirds were not uncommon, though parcels and long distance passenger traffic held up well. Lorries had also begun to eat into local freight traffic, though again long distance freight, particularly coal and other minerals, held up. Another long distance traffic that was well sustained was in homing pigeons. A special was noted in Banff in 1927; Banff and Fraserburgh were popular release points for pigeons from the south. Be that as it may, it was in fact freight traffic that was causing problems for the LNER, and indeed the other grouped companies. The recession of the late 1920s and early 1930s had hit heavy industry hard, and the problems of the north east of England in particular were hitting the LNER's finances very badly. It is little wonder then that it was looking for economies that would improve its financial situation.

The various grouped companies had obviously spent the first years of their existence in examining the viability of their various assets, and by the late 1920s would have taken note of their least viable passenger services. The axe began to fall, more or less nationwide, in 1930, and by 1931 it was obviously poised over the Oldmeldrum branch passenger service. The service had been run down over the previous few years, and had become of little use to anyone except those travelling to Aberdeen to catch main line connections southwards. Passenger services had declined to two services each way daily, leaving Inverurie at 8.50am and 4.48pm and returning from Oldmeldrum at 9.18am and 5.25pm; the goods service ran from Inverurie at 11am and returned from the terminus at 12.15pm.

In 1930 passenger receipts had totalled £243, which represented a loss in working of £718. When the loss of contributory revenue to main line services was taken into account, the savings from withdrawing the passenger service would be £514 per annum. This may seem a negligible amount to us today, but it was enough for the LNER to make arrangements for the withdrawal of passenger services. Parcels could still be conveyed by the goods trains and Alexander's buses would carry the mails. There had been few passengers travelling solely between Oldmeldrum and Inverurie, and there was no bus service between these two points. These would now be catered for by a skeleton service of two return trips between Fyvie, Oldmeldrum and Inverurie; passengers from Lethenty and Fingask could just about walk to stops on this route.

These considerations therefore led the LNER to issue notice of closure to passengers on the Oldmeldrum branch on and from Monday, 2nd November 1931. However, as there was no Sunday service on the branch, the last passenger train left Oldmeldrum at 5.25pm on Saturday, 31st October. Although the event did attract the attention of the local press, there were none of the demonstrations that such a closure would have evoked thirty years later. The Oldmeldrum shed, little used in latter years, was now officially closed. The daily goods service continued to run, operated either by a shunting engine or a locomotive running in after attention at Inverurie Works. This was the first closure of a passenger service on the Great North system since the

Class D40 No.6835 at Turriff in LNER days.   *(Keith Fenwick collection)*

A train waiting to leave Banff in the 1920s. The locomotive was D45 No.6851, originally class M No.51. It was withdrawn in January 1927 so, as was common practice, it was seeing out its days on light work such as the Banff branch. *(John Addison/GNSRA)*

closure of the Orton to Rothes section in 1866 and the diversion of trains from Waterloo to the Joint station at Aberdeen in 1867.

At this point, with the Oldmeldrum bay at Inverurie station now vacant, authority thought of using that for terminating the Macduff trains and closing Inveramsay, which had little local traffic. Its total income was £614 per annum as against staff wages of £1,079; staff pay had risen faster than the prices the railways could charge their customers. Such a proposal had been made previously, in 1870 and 1923, but had been rejected for various reasons. It fared no better this time as the locomotive works manager objected to using a shunting engine for manoeuvres at the station and, if tender engines were to continue in use on the Macduff branch, then a turntable would be required at Inverurie. The financial implications of all this caused the proposal to be dropped again. However, one economy that was effected on the Macduff branch in the 1930s was the closure of the crossing loops at Fyvie, Auchterless and King Edward.

By October, 1932, *Bradshaw* showed that the service on the Banff branch was now seven return trips per day. Timings were still about fifteen minutes for wholly passenger trains and twenty minutes for mixed; the latter accounted for about half the total. All trains now called at Ordens, permanently open since 1924, and 'when required' at Bridgefoot and Golf Club House halts. On the Macduff line the service was still five return trips per day, with all trains calling at all stations. The fastest trains now took just over one hour on the branch, though some took up to ten minutes longer to deal with any freight traffic. Also on the Macduff branch there were summer Sunday excursions from Aberdeen which had begun in 1926. These were advertised by weekly notice until 1938, when they began to appear in the timetables. A mystery from this period is why 38 first class tickets were issued at the closed stations of Lethenty and Oldmeldrum for £16 in 1937, and there were similar figures for 1938. Passengers could travel in the guard's van of freight trains on payment of first class fares; such a facility existed until

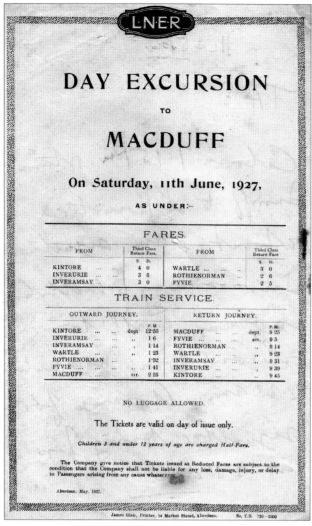

L·N·E·R

DAY EXCURSION

TO

MACDUFF

On Saturday, 11th June, 1927,

AS UNDER:—

FARES.

FROM	Third Class Return Fare.		FROM	Third Class Return Fare	
	S.	D.		S.	D.
KINTORE	4	0	WARTLE	3	0
INVERURIE	3	6	ROTHIENORMAN	2	6
INVERAMSAY	3	0	FYVIE	2	5

TRAIN SERVICE.

OUTWARD JOURNEY.				RETURN JOURNEY.			
			P.M				P.M.
KINTORE	dept	12·55	MACDUFF	dept.	8 25
INVERURIE	,,	1 6	FYVIE	arr.	9 5
INVERAMSAY	,,	1·14	ROTHIENORMAN	,,	9 14
WARTLE	,,	1 23	WARTLE	,,	9 23
ROTHIENORMAN	,,	1·32	INVERAMSAY	,,	9 31
FYVIE	,,	1 41	INVERURIE	,,	9 39
MACDUFF	arr.	2 25	KINTORE	,,	9 45

NO LUGGAGE ALLOWED.

The Tickets are valid on day of issue only.

Children 3 and under 12 years of age are charged Half-Fare.

The Company give notice that Tickets issued at Reduced Fares are subject to the condition that the Company shall not be liable for any loss, damage, injury, or delay to Passengers arising from any cause whatsoever.

Aberdeen, May, 1927.

James Blair, Printer, 24 Market Street, Aberdeen.   Sc. T.S. 730—2000

The inter-war period saw a marked rise in excursions such as this one in June 1927 to Macduff.

the 1960s throughout Scotland; passengers travelled at their own risk, even at first class fares! More likely, these were tickets booked for travel onwards from Inverurie, another facility which was offered at closed passenger stations which were still staffed.

By 1938 the summer service to Banff was eight return trips with an extra down on peak dates, while at Macduff the daily service was five trains, plus a late extra down on Saturdays. The summer Sunday service is shown in the public timetables as leaving Aberdeen at 1.45pm and arriving in Macduff at 3.20; it did not call at Inveramsay, Plaidy or King Edward. The up service left Macduff at 8pm and, omitting the same three calls, arrived at Aberdeen at 9.32. Also in 1938 the RCH *Handbook of Stations* noted that Oldmeldrum and Lethenty handled parcels and miscellaneous traffic but no passengers. Facilities were much the same elsewhere as in previous editions of the *Handbook*, except that motor cars rather than carriages could now be conveyed by passenger train. Additionally the 'Scottish Malt Distillers Ltd Inverboyndie Distillery' siding now had an entry; it would be used for bringing in coal and grain for the distillery as well as taking out the finished product.

A remarkable picture of life on the line in the 1920s and 1930s was given by Maurice Shand, who went on to serve the railways with distinction for another thirty years. His account of these times comes from the *Great North Review*, Nos 51, 52 and 54, in 1976 and 1977. Mr Shand had started his career on the Great North in 1920, when he held various posts in the Aberdeen area. However, later in the 1920s he was moved as clerk to Plaidy on the Macduff branch, then to Auchterless on the same line. He tells of the ambitions of the various staff wishing to climb the promotion ladder. Generally, if one was ambitious in that respect, it was necessary to move from station to station quite frequently, as Mr Shand did. Sometimes an apparent demotion was necessary. For instance Mr Shand tells of a chief goods clerk at Fraserburgh, a grade III station, accepting a station master's post at Auchterless, a grade V station; still a station master's job anywhere was prestigious enough, no matter where it was!

After various other travels Mr Shand became a relief telegraph clerk and spent some time in Turriff. He had earlier lived in the town, cycling daily from there to Plaidy and Auchterless. Then he was at Oldmeldrum just as the passenger service was withdrawn, though the livestock traffic was still considerable. By the time of World War 2 he was a relief station master and served at Turriff, which he found busy, though he thought Banff (Harbour) station 'a proper hole of a place'. Of course Mr Shand served at various stations and in ever more important posts outside the Banff and Oldmeldrum area as he went on to greater things, but his earlier career is typical of many who worked their way up through the railway hierarchy, doing many jobs at many stations; similar examples can be found in the records of the Great North and of other railways. There are examples too of others content to do the same job at the same place throughout their careers; for instance Alexander Dawson was crossing keeper at Mill of Boyndie from 1859 until 1905.

A group of workers at King Edward in LNER days.
(GNSRA collection)

War, Nationalisation and Another Closure

As in World War 1, when the second global conflict began in 1939 some railwaymen joined the forces at once. The immediate reaction to the declaration of war was a significant reduction in railway services. However, these were soon restored almost to pre-war levels, and by and large on the Banff and Macduff lines passengers could get around without too much trouble. Indeed as the war progressed and petrol rationing put a severe curb on private motoring, many former motorists were forced on to the railway if they had to get about, though the government tried to discourage any unnecessary travel. Normal freight traffic was just as much affected, as priority was given to the movement of war materials. Timber again was important of course, and was moved from various stations on the Macduff line.

More obvious military activity was to be seen near the Banff line. In 1942 an aerodrome was constructed to the west of Boyndie; it was locally referred to as Boyndie aerodrome, but its official title was RAF Banff. From there forays were made from 1943 onwards against the German forces in the Norwegian fjords. While this facility no doubt brought some traffic, both passenger and freight, to the railway, it had no direct connection. Indeed much of the airmen's cash seems to have been spent not on the railway but in the Railway Inn and other Banff hostelries! The aerodrome closed in 1946 and it is now a windfarm. The Macduff branch

Oldmeldrum in August 1958, looking towards Inverurie. The sidings were not overflowing but there are a couple of local lorries on the goods platform in the distance.   *(John A N Emslie)*

carried fuel oil to Turriff where a depot was built by the Ministry of Defence. This was piped to a concealed storage depot on the west side of the A947 for supply to local airfields.

However, as the war progressed and D-Day approached there were other pressures on the railways, and the little used station at Plaidy on the Macduff line closed completely on 22nd May, 1944.

Even when the war was over problems continued for the railways, still in the hands of the grouped companies. The winter weather in January to March 1947 was very severe throughout Britain. It was not so much the occasional snow blockage that was the problem, but a severe shortage of coal; there had been various problems in the pits, which had been nationalised at the start of that year. At that point the Macduff branch had four trains each way, one down from the five of the pre-war years, but by the summer timetable it was down to three. By 1948, however, the coal situation had eased and the service was back to four return trips, plus a Saturdays only trip from Macduff. Half of the trains ran through to/from Aberdeen, but the Sunday services had gone. At that time the service on the Banff branch was still six return trips with an extra each way on Saturdays.

By mid 1948 of course the railways had been nationalised, with all lines in Scotland coming under the control of the Scottish Region of British Railways. As at the grouping 25 years earlier, there were few immediate significant changes in liveries, services, facilities etc. However BR soon had a committee looking at unremunerative branch lines, and within two years another round of closures began. In particular BR frowned on localities being served by duplicate routes, even where the intermediate areas served were totally different, as was the case with the Banff and Macduff branches. When the services on the latter branch were again cut to three return trips, the writing was on the wall. Trains left Macduff at 6.40am, 12.20 and 5.10pm, and Inveramsay at 9.12am, 4.58 and 7pm. There was an early morning return goods trip from Kittybrewster to Macduff and one on Mondays only to Turriff. It was a classic case of running down a service ready for closure. Savings from closure to passengers were quoted by British

Railways as £5,000 per annum. Moreover matters were not helped by another coal shortage in early 1951, and the axe fell on passenger services to Macduff on and from Monday, 1st October of that year. In fact only the empty passenger stock was worked out of Macduff on that day, the service actually ceasing on the previous Saturday, 29th September. The rear of the last carriage of the last passenger train out of Macduff bore the chalked message: 'Ta! Ta! Macduff Gone For-ever!!!' The various protests had been of no avail, but the daily goods service continued. The locomotive depot was now closed, though the building was converted for storage purposes, and passenger driver Duff was moved to the distant Aberfeldy branch.

A rumour went around at the time that someone in the Scottish Region offices in Glasgow had become confused about the geography of Banff and Macduff, and that it was the Banff branch from Tillynaught that was intended for closure. Certainly it would seem that the Macduff branch had as good a case for survival as the Banff line had, at least as far as traffic was concerned. While it is not unknown for administrators to make such errors, the author rejects the rumour for two reasons. Firstly, as noted above, the passenger services on the Macduff branch had been run down over the previous few years to the extent that they were probably only useful for mail or, as with the Oldmeldrum example, for passengers wishing to make onward connections from Aberdeen. Secondly, the Macduff line was nearly thirty miles long whereas the Banff one was only six. The temptation to close down thirty miles to passengers was probably just too good to miss; again parallels can be found elsewhere.

Not that the Banff branch escaped the axe entirely, for by the mid 1950s even in summer the passenger service was down to four return trips daily plus two on Saturdays only; that was down from the 1950 service of seven return trips plus a Saturday extra. At least one traveller at that time speaks of the Banff trains carrying few if any passengers, thus bearing out the comments in the *Third Statistical Account*. Sunday School excursions appear to have operated regularly; long trains would run from Keith to Golf Club House, by then wholly a leisure facility. There was extra traffic for the Keith show in 1958. At this time another closure, but not one affecting the railway as such, was that of a station post office; there was one at Tillynaught Junction between 1949 and 1957. Be that as it may, once into the 1960s the closures really began.

Beeching and Beyond

An interesting development after the war had been the establishment of 'camping apartments' at Oldmeldrum and Macduff, probably from 1953 onwards. These were a development of the 'camping coaches', initiated between the wars, when coaches were parked at stations in holiday areas, such as Portessie and Portsoy, and were fitted up for families to stay for a week; they could use the adjacent station facilities for washing etc. By 1953 Oldmeldrum and Macduff stations were closed to passengers and so would have spare accommodation that could be turned into holiday apartments. A condition of occupancy was the purchase of rail tickets to the nearest station, presumably Inverurie and Banff in these cases. Oldmeldrum apartment survived until 1963 and Macduff untill 1962, which in fact was after the cessation of all traffic between Turriff and Macduff from 1st August, 1961. The daily freight service had departed Kittybrewster at 3.35am and had shunted at Macduff between 7.40 and 8.25; just in time to waken up the campers! By 1964, the service was in the hands of a 350hp diesel shunter (later Class 08) from Inverurie, leaving there at 6.10am. It was at the then terminus at Turriff between 8.35 and 9.55, and got back to Inverurie at 12.6pm. The Oldmeldrum freight was there between the rather more reasonable times, for the 1961 campers, of 11.20 and 11.55am. By 1964 a 204hp diesel (Class 06) left Inverurie at 12 noon to shunt at Oldmeldrum, and returned to base for 1.45pm.

By 1962, the Banff branch was the one remaining steam outpost in the north east and management was keen to introduce diesel traction. Diesel units were said to cost 4/- to 6/- (20p to 30p) per mile to operate, while steam trains cost 12/-, and while a diesel unit could have hauled a few wagons, it could not shunt them at Banff. It was proposed to work the branch by a Type 1 (later class 20) rather than a more expensive Type 2, but an independent source of heating would have been required. No solution to this problem seems to have been found but perhaps by then BR simply regarded the branch as doomed and thus not requiring a change in traction. Be that as it may, the writing was already on the wall for the Banff branch, for in a week in April of that year BR had carried out surveys on all its passenger lines with a view to reviewing, that is axing, unremunerative passenger services. The upshot of that exercise was the Beeching Report in March, 1963: *The Reshaping of British Railways*. Among other proposals it listed a large number of branches for closure to passenger services.

The Banff branch was indeed on that list, and it was also one of a number subjected to more detailed analysis. Its annual earnings from passengers were £800, which were expected to be lost totally if the line closed. It contributed £6,130 to the rest of the system, of which £4,000 were expected to be lost. Movement expenses were £14,150 per annum, which meant a saving of that sum less the £4,800 of lost revenue, should passenger services be withdrawn. When terminal expenses of £950 per annum and track and signalling expenditure of £600 were added in, the net gain from closure would be about £10,900 per annum. Some of these figures, such as the loss of contributory revenue, were open to question, but the Transport Users' Consultative

BR Standard Class 4 2-6-4Ts were popular on the lines in the north east and masters of their tasks. Here No.80020 is on a short train of empty cattle wagons on the up line at Turriff.   (A G Murdoch/GNSRA)

Miles	Week Days only	am	am	am	am	pm	pm	pm	pm	pm	pm
—	Aberdeen .... dep	..	7C 5	..	1015	..	..	2 10	..	3C55	6 20	
—	Tillynaught ... dep	7 15	8 56	1015	1155	1 5	3 0	3 45	4 50	5 55	8 15	..
1¼	Ordens Halt...	zz	zz	zz	zz	zz	zz	zz	zz	zz	zz	
3¼	Ladysbridge .	7 25	9 6	1021	12p1	1 15	3 6	3 51	4 56	6 1	8 21	
4¼	Bridgefoot Halt...	zz	zz	zz	zz	zz	zz	zz	zz	zz	zz	
5¼	Golf Club House Halt	zz	zz	zz	zz	zz	zz	zz	zz	zz	zz	
6	Banff .... arr	7 35	9 16	1030	1210	1 25	3 15	4 0	5 5	6 10	8 30	

Miles	Week Days only	am	am	am	am	pm	pm	pm	pm	pm	pm
—	Banff ... dep	6 45	8 30	9 50	1120	1230	2 30	3 23	4 25	5 25	7 50	
½	Golf Club House Halt ...	zz	zz	zz	zz	zz	zz	zz	zz	zz	zz	
1¼	Bridgefoot Halt ...	zz	zz	zz	zz	zz	zz	zz	zz	zz	zz	
2¼	Ladysbridge ...	6 52	8 37	9 57	1136	1246	2 37	3 30	4 32	5 32	7 57	
4¼	Ordens Halt	zz	zz	zz	zz	zz	zz	zz	zz	zz	zz	
6	Tillynaught .... arr	7 0	8 45	10 5	1145	1255	2 45	3 38	4 40	5 40	8 5	
—	Aberdeen .. arr	9 4	..	1150	..	..	4 38	..	6B49	..	9 48	

B Change at Cairnie Junction. On Saturdays arrives Aberdeen 6 51 pm
C Change at Cairnie Junction
zz All trains call to set down on request to guard or when there are passengers to take up

The final timetable for the Banff branch. In 1962 the train service was increased to ten each way to provide better connections at Tillynaught. Golf Club House was only open in the summer.

Committee for Scotland did not find enough hardship for users to accommodate such losses, and the branch was designated for closure.

Closure date was fixed for Monday, 6th July, 1964, though the last trains ran on the previous Saturday, 4th July; the branch did not even get a last season of summer traffic. While for some years an average of only 1½ passengers per train had been carried, the carriages were thronged on the last day; a report of events is carried in *Great North Review* No.2. The last train was doubled up from the usual two to four carriages and hauled by Class 2 No.78045. Its crew were long serving railwaymen, driver T. Ross and fireman J. Fraser. Even with four coaches the train was packed, and even the halts were crowded and produced more passengers. At 8.15pm the last down train left Tillynaught, again packed to the doors. Whistling all the way, the train arrived at a crowded Banff station. There were cheers and waves from both sides of the line, before the engine was uncoupled and run into its soon to be closed shed.

That left only goods services to Oldmeldrum, Turriff and Banff, although there were occasional passenger specials in the early and mid 1960s, usually run for enthusiast groups such as the Stephenson Locomotive Society and the Branch Line Society. The latter ran a railtour to Oldmeldrum, Alford and Turriff on 5th June, 1965, and its description of the trip describes facilities out of use or derelict, the lines being worked by the 'one engine in steam' principle, as the Oldmeldrum and Banff branches had usually been. The *RCH Handbook of Stations* for 1956 and its 1962 Appendix had indeed only shown a slight diminution of facilities at stations that were still open; however 'Horsebox' traffic had disappeared. Yet these goods services were not to go on forever, for 'Beeching' had also had something to say about freight services.

Though there were no long lists of freight closures, the Report concluded that loose coupled freight trains comprising small consignments of miscellaneous goods no longer had a place on British Railways. The maps in the Report showed that the stations on the three lines with which we are concerned each handled less than 5,000 tons of freight per annum, with the exception of Banff and Turriff which each handled between 5,000 and 25,000 tons. Consequently the Oldmeldrum and Turriff branches, along with the nearby branch to Alford, were officially closed completely from Monday, 3rd January, 1966, though the last trains had run on Hogmanay, 1965. However, a tanker which had earlier developed a fault was run to Turriff, where the oil depot was still in operation, on the Monday, but departed after discharge. The Oldmeldrum branch, which had received some television coverage on the Friday after closure, was then used for a time for wagon storage.

The Macduff and Oldmeldrum branches were visited on a few occasions by railtours in the 1960s. The final one, seen here at Oldmeldrum, was in June 1965 when the 2-coach railcar also went to Alford and Turriff. Some of the sidings had been lifted by then. (G N Turnbull/GNSRA)

The Banff branch, which had lost its signalling in July 1965 just after the passenger closure, now had a daily freight, something which it had seldom had before. However, this depended on the continuation of traffic on the 'Coast' line, whose closure had also been listed by 'Beeching'. Three routes between Aberdeen and Elgin were two too many as far as BR were concerned, and the shortest route, via Mulben, was kept, while those via Dufftown and via the Coast were closed completely as from Monday, 6th May, 1968; the last trains ran on Saturday, 4th May. The Banff freight service of course succumbed at the same time; there seems to have been little protest at it locally. Its freight service had been worked latterly by Type 2 diesels as part of a working from Keith to Buckie.

This might have seemed the end of railway activity in the Banff area, but in 1983 Mr Alan Sangster, who had been running a miniature railway near Cruden Bay, proposed moving it to Banff using the first mile of the branch's trackbed out from the site of the by then demolished Banff station, then diverting north west near to a caravan site at Swordanes. This new West Buchan railway, on fifteen inches gauge with steam and diesel traction, was opened on 23rd June, 1984. Although the venture seems initially to have been successful, it was apparently hit by bad weather later in the season. It seems to have reopened for the 1985 season, but closed by 31st August.

For the sake of completeness mention must also be made of a minor line nearby, close to Whitehills. This was at Blackpots, on the coast, where a brick, tile and pipe works had been established in 1766; the pipes were important in the drainage of the area. The clay for the works was extracted from a hillside to the south and wheeled in tubs by manpower over a narrow gauge line, of unknown gauge, to the works where it was tipped into chutes. The works continued until 1977, but the railway had apparently gone by then.

Chapter 6

Engineering

Locomotives

While the Oldmeldrum and Macduff branches were worked by the Great North from the beginning, the Banffshire Railway purchased its own locomotives and rolling stock. Its first two locomotives, 0-4-2Ts, were designed and built in 1859 by Hawthorn & Company of Leith and were numbered and named: 1 *Banff* and 2 *Portsoy*. In 1860 an 0-4-2 tender locomotive was purchased from Hawthorn, followed by another the following year. Their livery was green and the locomotive works was at Banff. Within a year of opening, the Banffshire found that they could not manage the maintenance of their locomotives. The Great North offered to undertake it and this was accepted in October 1860. When the GNS took over operations in 1863, they absorbed the locomotives in their own stock and renumbered them 37-40. Full details of these and all GNSR locomotives can be found in Hugh Gordon's *Great North of Scotland Railway Locomotives*.

Also at least one of the independent Morayshire Railway's first locomotives, numbered 1 and 2, seem to have worked at Oldmeldrum in the early days, though number 1 was withdrawn in 1859 and 2 in 1863, just after a brief run on the Oldmeldrum line. They were vertical boilered 2-2-0s designed by James Samuel. Perhaps the vertical boilers gave rise to early engines on the branch being referred to as 'coffee pots', a nickname quickly changed to 'Meldrum Meg', which was applied thereafter to all the locomotives and trains on the branch.

The Great North's first locomotive superintendent, Daniel Kinnear Clark, had designed

Class K No.45A at Kittybrewster. This was one of the engines which is known to have worked the Oldmeldrum branch. No doubt the tender cab would be welcomed on a branch where reverse running was involved.
(GNSRA collection)

twelve 2-4-0 tender engines for use on the original main line. These were built by Fairbairn of Manchester in 1854 and 1855 and one of these, number 4, had gravitated to the Oldmeldrum branch by 1857. Others from the 8 class, conceived as 0-6-0s but then built as 2-4-0s, appeared on the Macduff branch by 1880. Others from this batch and from those brought out by Clark's successor, John Folds Ruthven, in 1857 would also have appeared on the branches.

Ruthven's successor was William Cowan who, from 1862, established the 4-4-0 tender type on the Great North, one of the earliest examples of this wheel arrangement in Britain which was to dominate GNSR locomotive policy throughout its remaining history. Initially they would have run on main line passenger trains, but virtually all the 4-4-0 classes could be regarded as mixed traffic engines as they gravitated to other duties and to the various branches.

Apart from the early years, when all the Great North locomotives were relatively new, the three lines in our survey were worked by older engines seeing out their working lives on lighter duties. This particularly applied to the Oldmeldrum branch which could only be operated by 'third class' engines due to weight restrictions. One of Cowan's class B 2-4-0s is illustrated on page 4 when it must have been about 45 years old. One of the Class H 4-4-0s, built between 1862 and 1864, was at Oldmeldrum from about 1910 to 1915. No 35 of the same class was involved in the accident on the Macduff branch in 1882.

A slightly later Cowan design was the Class K of 1866. All six examples were known to have visited the Oldmeldrum branch and No.45 spent many years there, where of course it was known as *Meldrum Meg*. After 1916 44A was also seen at Banff. No.43 is illustrated at Ladysbridge on page 50.

Not that the weight restriction on the Oldmeldrum branch was always observed. A class M (D45) 4-4-0 of 1878 was spotted in 1913 at Oldmeldrum by the Great North's chief engineer,

Keeping with the tradition of using locomotives well past their prime on the branches in the north east, several ex-North British D34s were transferred to the area from 1953 and remained in use until 1960. No.62496 Glen Gloy is shunting at Rothienorman when working the 8.45am goods from Macduff on 15th August 1954. The signals here survived until the closure of the line.   (Transport Treasury)

Class 1 No.7 was one of the locomotives built for the opening of the Great North in 1854 and which proved suitable for the Oldmeldrum branch in its later life.   *(GNSRA collection)*

James Parker. He wrote formally to the locomotive superintendent, William Pickersgill, pointing out that the M class was barred from that branch; the latter was duly contrite. However, the class was admitted to the branch from 1928; it had also featured at Macduff in 1925.

A class C (D43) of 1879 was photographed at Ladysbridge on the Banff branch about 1909 and a class A (D44) of 1884 was seen at Oldmeldrum on 17th August 1925. The two class Ns (D46), which were the only locomotives built at Kittybrewster, were initially prohibited from the Banff, Macduff and Oldmeldrum branches, but were seen at Banff and Oldmeldrum after underbridges had been strengthened by the LNER in 1928. Class O (D42) of 1888 was initially intended for fast main line work, but No.72 was seen at Banff on 9th November 1916. Of the later main line 4-4-0s, classes S (D41), T (D41), V (D40) and F (D40), many examples worked the lines in later LNER days and in the early 1950s.

The Great North built a few tank engines, 0-6-0Ts and 0-4-4Ts, but they did not feature on our branches, although the lack of turntables at Banff and Oldmeldrum would have made them useful. However, some class R (G10) 0-4-4Ts appear to have been at Banff in the 1930s. The class X (Z4) 0-4-2Ts were designed and built by Manning, Wardle in 1915 for the Aberdeen Harbour lines. One of these, No.6844, was tried on the Oldmeldrum branch for a time, but with little success. This was probably because the trip to Oldmeldrum was a longer continuous run than shunting the harbour lines they were designed for and their short wheelbase would not take kindly to running at speed.

Gradually locomotives from the other companies that had made up the LNER found their way into Great North territory after 1923. Not surprisingly, ex-North British locomotives were the first to arrive in the form of D31 4-4-0s. Other NBR locomotives, such as the J36 0-6-0s, began to appear on the Macduff branch from about 1950 onwards; the LNER's own B1 4-6-0 mixed traffic engine 61348 was seen at Banff in 1950. Before then, from 1947 onwards, ex-North Eastern Railway G5 0-4-4Ts had begun to appear on the Banff branch and ex-NER J72 0-6-0Ts Nos 68750 and 68719 were noted at Oldmeldrum in 1954 and 1958 respectively. Nor was the London, Midland & Scottish unrepresented, for the Banff line featured some ex-Caledonian Railway McIntosh designed 0-4-4Ts in the 1950s, for instance '439' class No.55185 in June 1958, while a Fowler LMS 2P 4-4-0 was on the same line in 1959. Ex Caledonian 0-6-0 No.57591 was seen on the line in the summer of 1957.

From the early 1950s British Railways 'standard' designs also put in an appearance with

Standard 4MT 2-6-4Ts being noted at Turriff in the late 1950s, and of course the Standard 2MT 2-6-0s were the last steam passenger engines on the Banff branch, with No.78054 there in 1963 and No.78045 operating the last passenger services. Standard Class 4MT 2-6-0 No.76104 also worked the branch in June 1964.

Diesels were introduced in the area in 1960 and took over all workings, except the Banff branch, from July 1961. English Electric Type 1s (class 20) and North British Type 2s (class 21) were the main motive power along with the Sulzer engined type 2s (classes 24 and 26), plus various shunters. 204HP Barclay 0-4-0 diesels operated the Oldmeldrum branch goods in 1960. Diesels only appeared on the Banff branch after the passenger service was withdrawn, when the freight was worked as part of the Coast line service.

Rolling Stock

In the late nineteenth century, typical trains on the branches were made up as follows:

Banff: first, third, brake third, ten or more wagons;

Macduff: first, third, brake third, brake, five or six wagons;

Oldmeldrum: two composites, brake van, four wagons.

In the late 1940s a typical Macduff branch train was made up of a corridor or lavatory composite (GNS/LNER), and two non-corridor brake thirds (NER/LNER). Three such sets were required for the Macduff branch, and one for Banff. Composite carriages were much in demand for the branches, for a full bogie first would be somewhat of an over-provision for the surviving first class traffic.

Early carriages were four wheelers. It was not until the 1880s that six wheelers arrived on the main line and later on the branches; and it was the turn of the century before bogie carriages appeared on GNSR lines. By the new century electric lighting was in use on trains, though oil lamps continued into the 1930s on branch trains. Heating on branch line trains was by footwarmers for first class passengers only. The numbers of these that could be dealt with at one time at the various termini in the early twentieth century were as follows: Macduff – 32, Inveramsay – 16, Banff – 16, Oldmeldrum – 10. However, footwarmers, being in short supply, disappeared from most branches during World War 1. Another inconvenience for passengers

This four-wheeled coach, No.78 of diagram 28, dated from 1966 and was typical of those which worked the branches for most of the nineteenth century. By the early 1900s, coaches from the 1880s were in use, but four and six-wheelers survived until the 1930s.   *(GNSRA collection)*

was that stock on the branch lines was for the most part non-corridor.

The earliest livery for carriages was varnished teak, which Manson changed to crimson lake and Pickersgill to purple lake below and white at the windows. The LNER coach livery was varnished teak or brown, and the British Railways' one was red and cream, soon replaced by overall maroon. Those wishing full details of GNSR coaches, including liveries, should consult *Great North of Scotland Railway Carriages* by Keith Fenwick.

Rather surprisingly perhaps the Great North had no specialised fish vans. In 1883 a London interest, the Fish League, had designed such a van for use from the fishing ports to the London market. However, it proved unsuitable in use, and it was not until Grouping days that LNER-designed covered fish vans appeared in the Great North area. The GNSR had used normal closed vans or meat vans, or even open wagons to transport fish from such ports as Banff, Macduff and Fraserburgh.

The design of the signal box at Macduff was different from most other Great North boxes, with vertical planking and equal-sized windows. This is its condition in 1954. *(J L Stevenson)*

Civil Engineering

The Great North track eventually evolved into bull head rail, in up to sixty feet lengths, laid on sleepers set in granite chip ballast from Kemnay quarry on the Alford branch. We have already noted GNSR construction in Chapter 3 on the extension to Macduff. This of course was further developed over the years. Mileposts were usually on the downside of each branch and measured from Aberdeen; thus there was a 64½ milepost at Banff. Likewise bridges were numbered in sequence from Aberdeen over the main line, then over the various branches in sequence. For the Oldmeldrum branch the numbers were 341 to 352, for the Macduff line 361 to 445 and for Banff 451 to 467.

Trains running on GNSR track were, as noted earlier, controlled by a telegraph system whereby the progress of a train was authorised by telegraph messages from station to station. There had to be strict conformity to the regulations and the system was rather inflexible, but it was better than that which applied on some other companies' lines at the time. The Oldmeldrum branch had no train control system until 1895, being worked by the 'one engine in steam' principle.

The 1889 Railways Act, which dealt mainly with railway safety, brought changes in the 1890s. The block system, stipulated by the Act, meant that on single lines the driver had to have a token of some kind entitling him to be on a designated stretch of line and preventing another train being on that section. The Great North took some time to implement these regulations but gradually commissioned new signalling on the three branches during the 1890s.

Clearing up after the Inverythan accident of 1882. On the left are the remains of an open wagon carrying barrels. Several other wagons are strewn along the embankment side. A carriage body with its end torn off has been set upright on its wheels at ground level.   *(GNSR Association)*

There were of course bridges, cuttings and embankments on the three branches, and occasional trouble with these has already been noted. However, economy had dictated following the cheapest possible route; there were no major civil engineering works, such as tunnels and great viaducts, on the three branches. However a number of bridges were built of cast iron, which was cheaper than wrought iron, and this was to be the cause of a terrible accident on the Macduff branch; and so it is to the accidents on the three branches that we now turn.

Accidents

We have already mentioned two accidents which resulted in staff being injured, and there were others, such as a broken coupling at Turriff in 1876. In 1878, an axle broke on a train from Macduff about ½ mile north of Plaidy and most of the train derailed including the passenger coaches which were at the rear. Eight passengers were injured, but none seriously. This illustrated the danger of mixed trains as operated at that time. It is worth looking at three other accidents in more detail.

Class K No.45 had spent much of her life as 'Meldrum Meg' on that branch. Her adventures included demolishing the doors of the Oldmeldrum locomotive shed, then one dark night, according to A.M. Hardie, she was involved in a bizarre accident. A traction engine had fallen on to the railway line through an old wooden bridge near Inverurie; it should not have been on the bridge in any case. No.45 collided with the traction engine. Nobody was much hurt, but both engines were badly damaged. Indeed it was thought that No.45 might have to be scrapped, but she was patched up and went on to represent former Great North engines at the Stockton & Darlington Railway centenary celebrations in 1925.

There was a fatal accident at Mill of Boyndie level crossing in November 1901 when a tramp or poor workman, aged about seventy, somehow got marooned between the crossing gates without being noticed by the crossing keeper Alexander Dawson. The man was then run down and killed by an approaching train. Again accidents at level crossings involving trains and members of the public or their vehicles are still a major safety issue today.

However, a far more serious fatal accident had occurred at Inverythan on 27th November 1882. A train from Macduff had passed through Auchterless in poor weather and two miles south of there had crashed through a 35 feet span cast iron underbridge. The locomotive, recently rebuilt No.35, five tons heavier than the engines previously used on the branch, though derailed had passed over safely, but the five wagons at the head of the train crashed into the roadway. Worse still the front brake van, two third class carriages and one first class piled on top of the wreckage on the road; the rear brake van escaped unscathed. Four passengers died at the scene and another died later. Fourteen were injured, four seriously; fortunately for them a doctor was among the passengers. With regard to the number of casualties this was the worst accident in the Great North's history.

Major Marindin, who conducted the Board of Trade enquiry, found that the break had occurred in the southern half of the east girder, which had been cast in 1857 at Ferryhill Foundry, Aberdeen. The flaw could not have been found by normal inspection by staff, but more worrying was the fact that the Great North had 313 similar cast iron bridges, and the Major required immediate inspection and replacement by wrought iron structures where required. The fall of the cast iron Dee Bridge at Chester in 1847 had made such bridges suspect, though cast iron was still largely used in the first Tay Bridge, which had fallen in 1879. The Inverythan accident set even more alarm bells ringing about cast iron bridges, but even so metal fatigue is still an occasional cause of bridge failure on the railways.

Another bridge failure occurred in 1922, but this time fortunately without loss of life. On 18th April, a 6 ton Sentinel steam lorry and trailer carrying 7 tons 2cwt sacks of manure turned off the turnpike road from Turriff near Dounepark Farm. This crossed the line on an iron bridge with granite parapets and had a wooden surface which could not support the lorry. It fell on to the track. The 8.5am passenger train from Aberdeen was approaching but it managed to stop in time. The driver and attendant of the lorry managed to jump clear, but the driver's 15 year old son, who was also on the wagon, suffered a fractured leg. Passengers from this train and later ones had to alight at King Edward and walk or hire conveyances to Macduff. The Accident train arrived from Aberdeen later in the day to clear the line but a further mishap resulted in the jib of the crane striking the bridge and bringing down the iron parapets and masonry of the bridge. The driver claimed that he had looked for a sign indicating a weight limit on the bridge but had not seen one.

Fireman Fraser and a friend stand in front of No.78045 on the last day of passenger service at Banff.
(David Fraser)

Overline bridge on the Oldmeldrum branch, showing the simple construction employed in the 1850s. This example at OS reference NJ767238 was photographed in 1992.   (Keith Fenwick)

The stone building at Fyvie is the last survivor of the buildings there. It is not close to the sidings so was presumably used by one of the commercial firms which established distribution depots at various stations.   (Keith Fenwick)

Chapter 7

The Lines Today

This account of the Banff, Macduff and Oldmeldrum lines as they are today is based on exploratory walks made by the author over the last few years and on the most up to date maps available. Even where recent examination of sites has been made, the warning must be that situations can change quickly over a few months or even weeks! Another warning is that, while Scots law generally gives a wide range of access, care must be taken by anyone following the trackbeds to respect the privacy of those living in the buildings that are still extant.

While Inverurie station is still open for passenger traffic, the first half mile of the Oldmeldrum branch from the site of its divergence from the main line has been ploughed in. The site of Lethenty station (at Ordnance Survey Grid Reference NJ/769246) is covered by a timber yard used by the furniture manufacturers who now occupy Lethenty Mill; none of their buildings appear to be any part of the timber built Lethenty station. North of Lethenty the trackbed is walkable as far as the still discernible site of Fingask platform (NJ/778269). Thereafter it rather peters out and eventually disappears until Oldmeldrum is reached (NJ/804271). The station yard and building had long been the headquarters of an agricultural supply company,

Oldmeldrum station site is still recognisable as such. For many years, the station building was in use as offices but it has now been moved to Crathes where the Royal Deeside Railway Preservation Society have restored it. Several of the other buildings have been demolished.   *(Mike Cooper)*

After the closure of the Banff branch, the building at Ladysbridge was moved to nearby Whitehills, where it served as a pavilion for the adjacent sports field for many years. Eventually its condition deteriorated and it was replaced.
(Keith Fenwick)

but in 2011 the timber station building was removed in pieces to Milton of Crathes on the preserved Royal Deeside line where it has been re-erected and restored. The yard is now used for bus storage and the Aberdeen Commercial Company's warehouse has been adapted for commercial use.

At the junction of the Macduff branch with the main line at Inveramsay (NJ/736253) there is little to see in the way of buildings, though the trackbed is still easily traceable to the first station on the branch, Wartle (NJ/720303). It, like Rothienorman, Fyvie and Auchterless, was built of brick in 'house style' adopted by the Aberdeen & Turriff Railway. Wartle station, now harled, and Auchterless (NJ/747443), also harled, are dwelling houses. Rothienorman station (NJ/723356) has gone, while Fyvie station was initially used as a store, but fell derelict and was demolished about 1996, though a stone shed remains as a store among modern buildings (NJ/758390). The trackbed continues reasonably intact through Rothienorman and Fyvie, though most of the underbridges were removed in the 1970s, the track itself having gone soon after complete closure. However, the trackbed peters out near Inverythan, the site of the 1882 tragedy, and is only intermittently visible to within a mile or so of Turriff. Then it reappears, only to disappear again for a mile or more through the town. The last vestige of the substantial station buildings at Turriff was the signal box, which was demolished in 1978; a storage shed survives (NJ/725494) together with the edge of the goods platform.

North of Turriff the trackbed can be traced through Plaidy to King Edward. These two stations and Banff Bridge were timber built. At Plaidy (NJ/730549) the agent's house is still in use, though the station itself has gone. King Edward station buildings are extant (NJ/717580). For a time they were obscured by modern additions, but these have now been removed and some renovation undertaken, though the future of the building still seems uncertain. It no longer houses the post office, where in 1936, during the abdication crisis, much business was done franking letters with the 'King Edward' postmark. After a gap north of King Edward the trackbed becomes easily traceable, though with some breaks, until the outskirts of Macduff. Along the south side of the Hill of Doune the trackbed is somewhat overgrown, but the site of the original Banff and Macduff station can still be traced (NJ/697635). Then comes Banff Bridge station, whose original timber building now forms a 'pebble dash' walled house (NJ/696636). The nearby embankment was eroded by floods in 1995, but the station was in no immediate danger. At the end of another stretch of intact trackbed the overall roofed, stone built Macduff station and carriage shed still exists as the warehouse of a boat builder and fishing industry supply company (NJ/701643). Moreover the engine shed still survives, apparently now used as a workshop after a period as a store. These extant buildings are a reminder of the long trudge uphill to the station for passengers, and horses and carts, which in the end did little good for its traffic prospects.

At Tillynaught on the 'Coast' line, the site of the junction for the Banff branch can be traced, though nothing remains of the station (NJ/601617). The trackbed is largely intact right through to Banff. The last mile into Banff, used for a time in the 1980s by the West Buchan Railway, is now an official footpath. The branch's stations have not been so fortunate, however. Ladysbridge station site (NJ/651637) is now covered by houses, though the station building itself was removed to Whitehills to form, for about forty years until a recent functional replacement, a pavilion for the local football club. The halts too, at Ordens (NJ/623622), Bridgefoot (NJ/670645) and Golf Club House (NJ/677645), have largely vanished. Banff Harbour station and carriage shed was stone built and had an overall roof, like Portsoy at the other terminus of the Banffshire Railway; and, like Macduff, Portsoy has survived, this time as an agricultural warehouse. However, Banff station (NJ/688647), after some years of dereliction, was demolished in the 1970s, though the site is still empty, and the track of the harbour extension can still be traced to its terminus on a quay (NJ/689646).

So how do the inhabitants of the various locations on the three branches now get around, should they need to use public transport?

There is now an hourly bus service between Aberdeen and Oldmeldrum, Turriff, Macduff and Banff; with the hourly service going on to Elgin via Ladysbridge and Whitehills, and even on to Inverness, as the trains once did. There are also extra local buses between Macduff, Banff, Ladysbridge and Whitehills, and between Aberdeen and Oldmeldrum. Aberdeen to Banff by road, a distance of 46 miles, is now covered by the bus in 1 hour 55 minutes; whereas the train had to cover 64½ miles, typically in 2h10m, of course with a change of train at Tillynaught. Macduff, also 46 miles by road from Aberdeen, is reached by the bus in 1h45m, while the best trains took 1h40m, but longer when a change of train was needed at Inveramsay. Oldmeldrum is only eighteen miles from Aberdeen by road, as against 22 miles by rail. The bus takes 55 minutes, but the change of train at Inverurie pushed the train time up to about 1h10m. Thus in general the bus times are shorter than the train ones over the same routes and the frequency is much better. Moreover, the buses pass through the centre of the towns, whereas the rail termini at Banff, Macduff and Oldmeldrum were situated at the edge.

On the stretch of the Macduff branch not served by the A947 road, that is between the

For many years, the station building at King Edward was hidden behind assorted items but the site has now been cleared and it can be seen properly. While much of it is plain, there are some attractive details.

(Brenda Duncan/ GNSRA)

The view today looking south at the site of Turriff station. The road to Aberdeen can be seen on the far right. The photographer is standing on the site of part of the up platform; part of its wall is to the left of the roadway into the caravan park which occupies much of the site.   *(Mike Cooper)*

junction at Inveramsay and Fyvie, the villages of Wartle and Rothienorman are now served by six buses on weekdays from Inverurie, with three going on via Kirkton of Auchterless to Turriff. The change of bus at Inverurie is a cause of delay and the Aberdeen to Rothienorman journey can take up to an hour and a half, as against just over one hour by the through trains. However, Oldmeldrum now has virtually an hourly service to Inverurie, but Lethenty is served by the Inverurie to Rothienorman buses. Another warning: these bus services are as at the time of writing, and are liable to sudden and significant changes!

About one hundred and eighty years ago the Aberdeen to Banff turnpike road had afforded 'both an economical and expeditious mode of travelling' between the two places. One hundred years ago the Great North of Scotland Railway had usurped that claim very emphatically. However, after 1918 road traffic, whether private or public, began to displace that of the railway. The latter suffered from various problems. Passengers, and to some extent freight customers, found rail charges generally uncompetitive compared with those by road, though there were exceptions; bus services were usually more frequent; rail transport often involved travel by roundabout routes, sometimes with time consuming and inconvenient changes of train at remote junctions; similarly freight traffic by rail sometimes involved costly and time-consuming 'double handling'; and stations were sometimes at some distance from the settlements which they purported to serve.

Of course the three branch lines described above, which variously suffered from most if not all of the above problems, were not alone; branch lines elsewhere were similarly afflicted. However, they were particularly hit by the convenience and directness of the trunk road, now the A947, so that in effect the transport system in the places along its line has reverted to that of one hundred and eighty years ago; the main difference from that time being that Stagecoach has now replaced the stagecoach!

Appendix : Stations and Signal Boxes

Oldmeldrum Branch

Name	Dist	OS Ref	Opened Passenger	Opened Goods	Closed Passenger	Closed Goods
Inverurie	0 00					
Lethenty	1 67	NJ 769 245	1 11 1856	6 7 1856	2 11 1931	6 2 1961
Muirtown	2 75	NJ 773 263				
Fingask	3 49	NJ 778 268	by 1867		2 11 1931	
Oldmeldrum	5 07	NJ 803 270	1 7 1856	6 7 1856	2 11 1931	3 1 1966

Macduff Branch

Name	Dist	OS Ref	Opened Passenger	Opened Goods	Closed Passenger	Closed Goods
Inveramsay	0 00					
Glenlogie Siding	1 40	NJ 722 269				
Wartle	3 48	NJ 720 301	5 9 1857	5 9 1857	1 10 1951	10 8 1964
Rothienorman	7 28	NJ 723 356	5 9 1857	5 9 1857	1 10 1951	3 1 1966
Fyvie	10 47	NJ 757 390	5 9 1857	5 9 1857	1 10 1951	3 1 1966
Auchterless	14 00	NJ 746 443	5 9 1857	5 9 1857	1 10 1951	10 8 1964
Turriff	17 66	NJ 724 493	5 9 1857	5 9 1857	1 10 1951	3 1 1966
Plaidy	22 18	NJ 729 549	4 6 1860	4 6 1860	22 5 1944	22 5 1944
King Edward	24 42	NJ 716 578	1 3 1861	4 6 1860	1 10 1951	1 8 1961
Macduff (1st location)	29 09	NJ 698 634	1 3 1861	4 6 1860	1 7 1872	1 7 1872
Banff Bridge	29 29	NJ 696 677	1 7 1872		1 10 1951	
Macduff (2nd location)	29 64	NJ 700 642	1 7 1872	1 7 1872	1 10 1951	1 8 1961

Banff Branch

Name	Dist	OS Ref	Opened Passenger	Opened Goods	Closed Passenger	Closed Goods
Tillynaught	0 00					
Ordens	1 56	NJ 622 621	1 10 1859		6 7 1964	
Ladysbridge	3 54	NJ 651 636	1 10 1859	1 10 1859	6 7 1964	6 5 1968
Boyndie	4 65	NJ 667 642		By 1867		Before 1968
Bridgefoot	5 00	NJ 670 644	1 10 1913		6 7 1964	
Golf Club House	5 34	NJ 677 644	1 10 1913		6 7 1964	
Banff (Temporary Terminus)			30 7 1859	30 7 1859	1 5 1860	1 5 1860
Banff	6 13	NJ 687 646	1 5 1860	1 5 1860	6 7 1964	6 5 1968

Signal Boxes

Name	Type	Opened	Closed	Notes
Oldmeldrum	2b	3 6 1895	2 11 1931	Retained as ground frame
Rothienorman	2b	24 12 1894	11 12 1961	
Fyvie	2b	15 4 1895	5 10 1936	
Auchterless South	2b	28 3 1892	28 3 1933	
Auchterless North	2b	28 3 1892	28 3 1933	
Turriff	3a	12 8 1900	11 12 1961	
King Edward	2b	29 4 1895	6 1 1936	
Macduff	-	29 4 1895	1 8 1961	
Banff	2a	3 12 1900	29 3 1960	

Bibliography

Minute Books of the Great North of Scotland Railway, Banffshire Railway, Aberdeen & Turriff Railway and Banff, Macduff & Turriff Extension Railway in the National Records of Scotland, General Register House, Edinburgh

Board of Trade Inspection Reports

Directors, Dilemmas and Debt, Peter Fletcher, GNSRA, 2010

Great North Review, Great North of Scotland Railway Association

Great North Memories, The British Railways Era, GNSRA, 2014

Great North of Scotland Railway - A Guide, W Ferguson of Kinmundy, David Douglas, 1881

Great North of Scotland Railway (2nd Edition), H A Vallance, House of Lochar, 1989

Great North of Scotland Railway Carriages, Keith Fenwick, Black Dwarf Lightmoor, 2009

Great North of Scotland Railway Locomotives, Hugh Gordon, Irwell Press, 2008

History of the Great North of Scotland Railway, Sir C M Barclay-Harvey, Ian Allan.

New Statistical Account of Scotland

Regional History of the Railways of Great Britain, Vol.15, J Thomas & D Turnock, House of Lochar. 1989

The Book of Banff, Banff Preservation & Heritage Society, Halsgrove, 2008

Third Statistical Account of Scotland

Great North of Scotland Railway Association

Founded 1964

Dedicated to keeping the memory of the 'Little and Good' alive, the Association caters for all those interested in the history of the Company and its constituents, as well as the lines during the LNER, British Railways and post-privatisation periods. The Association promotes the study and collection of information, documents and illustrations relating to all aspects of the North East's railways. It also facilitates and co-ordinates members' research and provides information for modellers.

Members receive a quarterly *Review* containing articles, photographs, drawings and news of the railway, both historical and current. The Association has produced a comprehensive range of books and technical papers covering aspects of the railway in great detail. Members have access to an extensive photographic and drawing archive, and receive a discount on Association publications. Meetings and excursions are regularly organised.

For further information, please look at the Association's website www.gnsra.org.uk.

Rear Cover Illustrations

(Upper) The final chance for enthusiasts to travel over the Oldmeldrum and Turriff branches was on a railtour on 5th June 1965 which also visited Alford. The return working from Turriff is seen here at Fyvie, where the crew patiently waited for photographs to be taken and the station to be explored.

(G N Turnbull)

(Lower) Of all the stations described in this book, more remains of the original structure at Macduff than anywhere else. The solid stone buildings have gradually been adapted to their new use by the Seaway Group which builds and repairs fishing boats and supplies fishing equipment. The main station building in the distance has been substantially rebuilt but its original form is evident. The locomotive shed is in the centre foreground, while the other buildings are new.   *(Courtesy Seaways Group)*